Stylish Jewelry
Your Way

Designs in
stringing, wirework, stitching, metalwork, and more

Compiled by Karin Van Voorhees

KALMBACH BOOKS

Kalmbach Books
21027 Crossroads Circle
Waukesha, Wisconsin 53186
www.Kalmbach.com/Books

Published in 2014
18 17 16 15 14   1 2 3 4 5

Manufactured in China

ISBN: 978-1-62700-073-4
EISBN: 978-1-62700-105-2

Editor: Karin Van Voorhees
Art Director: Carole Ross
Illustrator: Kellie Jaeger
Photographers: William Zuback, Jim Forbes

Publisher's Cataloging-in-Publication Data

Stylish jewelry your way : designs in stringing, wirework, stitching,
  metalwork, and more / [compiled and] edited by Karin Van Voorhees.

   p. : col. ill. ; cm. + 1 DVD (sd., col. ; 4 3/4 in.)

"The material in this book has appeared previously in *Beautiful Jewelry Make It Wear It, Bead&Button,*
  or *Bead Style* magazines."—T.p. verso.
Accompanying DVD features 28 technique tutorials.
Issued also as an ebook.
ISBN: 978-1-62700-073-4

1. Jewelry making—Handbooks, manuals, etc. 2. Beadwork—Handbooks, manuals, etc.
3. Wire jewelry—Design—Handbooks, manuals, etc. 4. Metal-work—Handbooks, manuals, etc.
I. Van Voorhees, Karin. II. Title: Bead&Button magazine. III. Title: Bead style. IV. Title: Beautiful jewelry.

TT212 .S79 2014
745.594/2

Contents

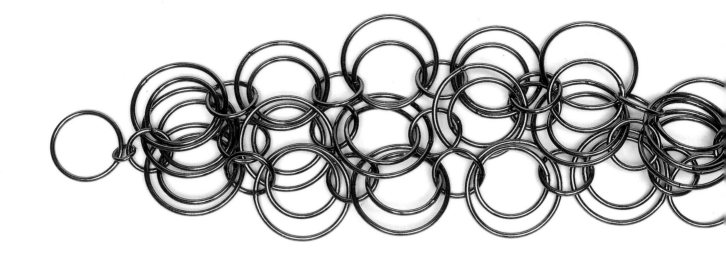

Stylish Jewelry *Your Way*

Why do we make jewelry? Is it the creative expression? The joy that comes with using our hands to shape a miscellaneous collection of beads and findings into a beautiful, cohesive statement piece? Do we revel in a few minutes of quiet and focused concentration as a detour from our demanding lives? Or do we simply want to enhance our wardrobes with a perfect made-our-way accessory?

For many, it's all of the above. We love to create, to experiment with new techniques and materials, and to wear what we've made. We love the control that comes with making something ourselves, and how our choice of colors or materials can be an extension of our personal styles. Speaking of style, it can be as multifaceted as the crystals we string with: tailored for the office, romantic for special occasions, a little bohemian on the weekends, and edgy for a night on the town with friends.

Browse through *Stylish Jewelry Your Way* and think of your lifestyle. Is there a piece you can make to go with a new outfit, or wear on an upcoming occasion? Don't worry if you've never tried some of the techniques like stitching, metalworking, or wireworking. Choose the jewelry you want to make, and the easy step-by-step directions will guide you. If you need to brush up on skills before you begin, everything you need to know to complete these projects is explained in Basics (p. 89). Still not sure? Check out the bonus DVD: Kalmbach jewelry magazine editors give you up-close demonstrations of 28 jewelry-making techniques. Check for this symbol ⊙ in the materials list and the Basics section for a quick reference of DVD topics.

Grab your supplies, pick a project (or a few), and join the fun of making beautiful and stylish jewelry *your way*.

Romantic Allure

Sweet and beautiful, this jewelry is designed to enhance your softest, most romantic look. Using materials such as pearls, flowers, ribbon, delicate filigree, and jewel-toned crystals and beads, you'll create jewelry to flatter your feminine side. Stitch a chevron chain, string rounds and rounds of pearls, or try your hand at wireworking to make your own romantic accessories.

Briolettes on parade

Toni Taylor shows us how two strands of beads take on a whole new look when you connect clusters of crystals and add an edging of briolettes. Metallic beads set off the romantic shades and provide a bright contrast.

materials

bracelet 7½ in. (19.1 cm)

- **26** 5 mm cubic zirconia briolettes or other drop-shaped beads
- **52** 4 mm bicone crystals
- **119** 2 mm round beads or 11º seed beads
- **24–28** 2.1–3 mm tube beads or bugle beads
- lobster claw clasp
- **2** 4 mm soldered jump rings
- **4** mm jump ring
- Fireline 6 lb. test

tools & supplies

- Stitching Toolbox, p. 89
- Stringing Toolbox, p. 89

techniques

- beadweaving

DVD review ▶

- Stitching: Ending and Adding Thread
- Stringing: Opening and Closing Jump Rings

1. On 2 yd. (1.8 m) of Fireline, pick up a 2 mm round bead and a soldered jump ring, leaving a 6-in. (15 cm) tail. Sew back through the 2 mm.

2. Pick up a 2.1–3 mm tube bead, a 2 mm, a 4 mm bicone crystal, a 2 mm, a 4 mm, and a 2 mm. Repeat this pattern 12 times, then pick up a tube, a 2 mm, and a soldered jump ring, and sew back through the last 2 mm.

3. Pick up a tube, a 2 mm, and a 4 mm. Sew back through the 2 mm between the last pair of 4 mms in the previous strand **(figure a, a–b)**. Pick up a 4 mm, a 2 mm, a tube, a 2 mm, and a 4 mm. Sew through the 2 mm between the next pair of 4 mms in the previous strand **(b–c)**. Repeat the pattern to **point d**.

4. Pick up a 4 mm, a 2 mm, and a tube. Sew through the end 2 mm in the previous strand and the soldered jump ring. Sew back through the end 2 mm, and continue through the first tube and 2 mm picked up in the first strand **(d–e)**.

5. Sew diagonally through the next 4 mm on this strand, the shared 2 mm between the strands, and the opposite 4 mm on the other strand **(figure b, a–b)**. Pick up a 2 mm, a briolette, and a 2 mm, and sew through the previous 4 mm on this strand and the shared 2 mm **(b–c)**. Retrace the thread path of the briolette embellishment, exiting again at **point c**.

6. Sew through the next 4 mm on the other strand **(c–d)**. Pick up a 2 mm, a briolette, and a 2 mm, and sew through the previous 4 mm on this strand and the shared 2 mm **(d–e)**. Retrace the thread path of the briolette embellishment,

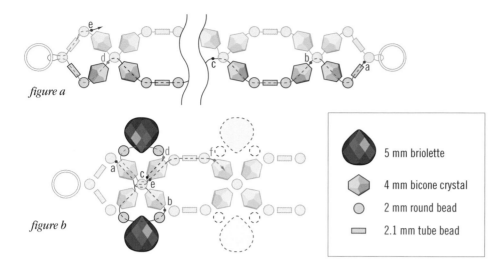

figure a

figure b

◆	5 mm briolette
⬡	4 mm bicone crystal
●	2 mm round bead
▭	2.1 mm tube bead

Don't pull the thread too tight in the first strand. A medium tension will allow the crystals to form even clusters when you sew through the shared 2 mms between the strands.

and continue through the next 4 mm, 2 mm, tube, and 2 mm on this strand (**e–f**).

7. Repeat steps 5 and 6 for the length of the bracelet, and end the working thread and tail (Stitching Basics, p. 89).

8. Open a 4 mm jump ring (Stringing Basics, p. 89), and attach a lobster claw clasp to the soldered jump ring on one end of the bracelet. Close the jump ring.

Budget *option*

Affordable fill-ins. To cut back on costs, substitute pressed-glass petals for the cubic zirconias, 11° seed beads for the 2 mm round beads, and 3 mm bugle beads for the 2.1 mm tube beads.

Wired for beauty

A handmade art-glass bead sparked the design for this easy wirework choker by **Linda Augsburg**, finished with a handmade clasp. To customize it, try different combinations of beads: Change the look dramatically with a round focal bead accented by clusters of dangles in complementary, rather than coordinating, colors.

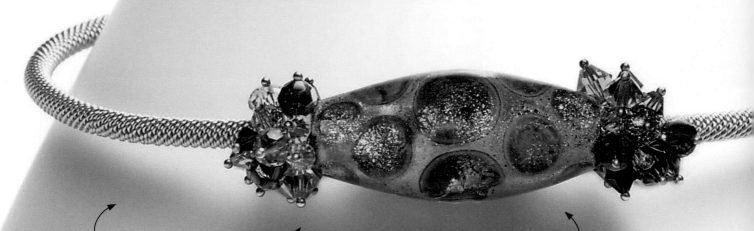

Choker

1. Cut two 6-ft. (1.8 m) pieces of 22-gauge (0.64 mm) twisted wire and an 18-in. (46 cm) piece of 16-gauge (1.29 mm) wire. Coil one twisted wire around the 16-gauge core wire (Wirework Basics, p. 91). Repeat with the second twisted wire. Remove the coils from the core.

2. String a crystal on a head pin, and make a wrapped loop (Wirework Basics). Repeat to make 35 more dangles.

3. Center an art-glass bead on the core wire, and string an equal number of dangles on each end. Curve the core wire to fit your neck, and determine the desired finished length. String a coil on each end of the core wire, and trim an equal length from each coil to fit the desired length, if necessary. Don't trim the core wire yet.

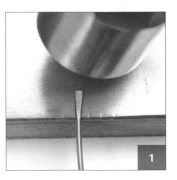

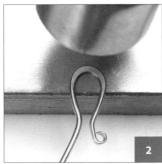

1

2

3

A built-in hook-and-eye clasp makes for a pretty finish.

materials

choker 18½ in. (47 cm)

- 12 ft. (3.7 m) 22-gauge (0.64 mm) twisted gold-filled wire
- 18 in. (46 cm) 16-gauge (1.29 mm) round gold-filled wire, half-hard
- 40 mm art-glass bead
- **36** crystals in assorted shapes, sizes, and colors
- **36** 22- or 24-gauge decorative head pins

tools & supplies

- Wirework Toolbox, p. 91

techniques

- wirework
- stringing

DVD review ▶

- Wirework: Wrapped Loop

Clasp

1. Slide the components to one end of the core wire. Using a chasing hammer, hammer the opposite end of the core wire on a bench block or anvil to form a ³⁄₁₆-in. (5 mm) paddle **(photo 1)**.

2. Using roundnose pliers, form the paddle into a small loop. Grasp the core wire about ¾ in. (1.9 cm) from the loop, and bend the wire over the pliers to form a hook. Hammer the top of the hook to harden it **(photo 2)**.

3. Using roundnose pliers, grasp the core wire below the hook, and make a second small loop facing opposite the first loop. Hammer the second loop.

4. Slide the components to the hook end of the choker. Cut the core wire 2 in. (5 cm) beyond the end of the coil. Using roundnose pliers, make a large loop perpendicular to the hook, leaving a ¼-in. (6 mm) tail. Slide the coil away from the loop, and hammer the loop **(photo 3)**. Slide the coil over the loop's tail. Shape the choker to fit your neck.

Note from Linda: The beautiful art bead I used for this necklace was purchased at the Bead&Button Show several years ago and I don't know if it is still available. There are a million beautiful art beads looking for a home in your necklace, though, so happy art-bead shopping!

Make sure the bench block and hammer face are smooth; any texture will transfer to the wire when you hammer it.

Budget *option*

Wallet-friendly wire. Gold-filled wire is gorgeous, no doubt, but you need a little over 13 ft. (4 m) of it for this project. Try brass wire instead; you'll get the warm look of gold without the steep price tag.

Fantastic chevron chain

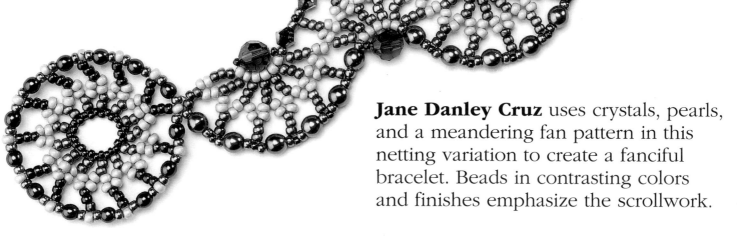

Jane Danley Cruz uses crystals, pearls, and a meandering fan pattern in this netting variation to create a fanciful bracelet. Beads in contrasting colors and finishes emphasize the scrollwork.

Chevron chain

1. On a comfortable length of Fireline, attach a stop bead (Stitching Basics, p. 89), leaving a 6-in. (15 cm) tail. Pick up three color A 11º seed beads, two color B 11º seed beads, three As, a B, three As, and two Bs, and sew back through the first three As picked up (**figure a, a–b**).

2. Pick up a color C 11º seed bead, a 4 mm pearl, a C, three As, and two Bs, and sew back through the last three As added in the previous stitch (**b–c**).

3. Pick up a B, three As, and two Bs, and sew back through the three As added in the previous stitch (**c–d**).

4. Repeat steps 2 and 3 four times (**d–e**), then repeat step 2 (**e–f**).

5. Pick up a C, a 4 mm bicone crystal, a C, three As, and two Bs, and sew back through the three As added in the previous stitch (**f–g**).

6. Repeat steps 3 and 5 (**g–h**) five times.

7. Repeat steps 2–6 twice, ending and adding thread as needed (Stitching Basics).

Embellishment

1. Sew back through the last six Bs added along this edge. Pick up a 15º seed bead, a 6 mm round crystal, and a 15º, and sew through the six Bs again (**figure b, a–b**). Sew through the next C, 4 mm, and C along the edge (**b–c**).

2. Pick up a 15º, and sew through the next C, 4 mm, and C (**c–d**). Repeat this step four times.

3. Repeat steps 1 and 2 twice. Remove the stop bead, and sew through the beadwork to the other edge of the bracelet. Work as in steps 1 and 2 to embellish the other edge of the bracelet, then end the working thread and tail.

Toggle bar

1. On 20 in. (51 cm) of Fireline, attach a stop bead, leaving a 6-in. (15 cm) tail.

2. Pick up 18 15ºs. Work in flat even-count peyote stitch (Stitching Basics) for a total of 10 rows. You will have five 15ºs along each straight edge of the band. Zip up (Stitching Basics) the ends to form a tube.

3. Sew through the center of the tube, and pick up a 4 mm round crystal and a 15º. Skip the 15º, and sew back through the 4 mm and the center of the tube to exit the other end.

4. Repeat step 3, and retrace the thread path several times. Sew through the beadwork, and exit a 15º in the middle of the toggle bar.

5. Pick up six As, a 4 mm bicone crystal, and five As, and sew

- ⬡ 6 mm round crystal
- ⬤ 4 mm Czech glass pearl
- ⬢ 4 mm bicone crystal
- ⬤ 3 mm Czech glass pearl
- ● 11º seed bead, color A
- ○ 11º seed bead, color B
- ● 11º seed bead, color C
- ● 11º seed bead, color D
- • 15º seed bead

Give it some glass. For a budget-friendly option, substitute fire-polished and Czech glass beads for the crystals and pearls. Choose bright colors to give you the same show-stopping look.

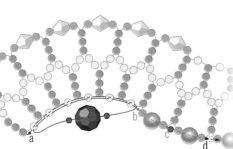

figure a

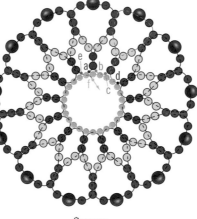

figure b

figure c

materials

bracelet 7¾ in. (19.7 cm)

- **6** 6 mm round crystals (Swarovski, amethyst)
- **18** 4 mm Czech glass pearls (purple)
- **19** 4 mm bicone crystals (Swarovski, crystal dorado 2X)
- **2** 4 mm round crystals (Swarovski, purple velvet)
- **13** 3 mm Czech glass pearls (burgundy)
- 11º seed beads in each of **4 colors:**
  - 10 g color A (Miyuki 460, medium gold metallic iridescent)
  - 10 g color B (Toho 557F, matte galvanized starlight)
  - 1 g color C (Miyuki 4213, dark mauve)
  - 1 g color D (Miyuki 466, deep brown metallic iridescent)
- 1 g 15º seed beads (Miyuki 454, dark purple iridescent)
- Fireline 6 lb. test

tools & supplies

- Stitching Toolbox, p. 89

techniques

- chevron chain

DVD review ▶

- Stitching: Ending and Adding Thread

through the first A on one end of the bracelet. Pick up four As, and sew through the first A added after the 4 mm bicone crystal, the 4 mm bicone crystal, and the next A. Pick up five As, and sew through the 15º in the toggle bar your thread exited at the start of this step. Retrace the thread path, and end the working thread and tail.

Toggle ring

1. On 1 yd. (.9 m) of Fireline, pick up 26 15ºs, leaving a 6-in. (15 cm) tail. Sew through the first 15º to form a ring.

2. Pick up two As, two Bs, three color D 11º seed beads, a C, a 3 mm pearl, a C, three Ds, and two Bs, and sew back through the first two As picked up at

the start of this stitch (**figure c, a–b**). Skip the next 15º in the original ring, and sew through the following 15º (**b–c**).

3. Pick up two As and two Bs, and sew back through the last three Ds picked up in the previous stitch. Pick up a C, a 3 mm pearl, a C, three Ds, and two Bs, and sew back through the pair of As picked up at the start of this step. Skip a 15º in the original ring, and sew through the following 15º in the ring (**c–d**).

4. Repeat step 3 11 times, but in the last repeat, after the C, 3 mm pearl, and C, sew through the adjacent three Ds added in the first stitch to join the ends. Pick up two Bs, and sew back

through the last two As added (**d–e**). Skip the next 15º in the original ring, and sew through the following 15º (**e–f**). Sew through the beadwork to exit a C, 3 mm, and C along the outer edge of the ring.

5. Pick up a B, and sew through the next C, 3 mm, and C. Repeat around the ring, and exit a B along the outer edge.

6. Sew through an A on the remaining end of the bracelet, then sew back through the B your thread exited at the start of this step. Retrace the thread path to secure, and end the working thread and tail.

Bracelet in bloom

To make a colorful cuff, **Naomi Fujimoto** adds a stack of Lucite roses to memory wire strung with crystals. Buy a few flower sets and layer different colors, or stick with a monochromatic set that matches one of the crystals. Use gold spacers liberally to lend an air of opulence to this permanent corsage.

1. On a head pin, string a 3 mm flat spacer, the layers of a Lucite rose from smallest to largest, and a 3 mm flat spacer. Make a wrapped loop (Wirework Basics, p. 91, and **photo 1**).

2. Using heavy-duty wire cutters or memory-wire cutters, cut a six- or seven-coil piece of memory wire. On one end, use roundnose pliers to make a loop (Wirework Basics). String two 4 mm spacers, a color A 6 mm bicone crystal, two 4 mm spacers, a color B 6 mm bicone, a 3 mm flat spacer, an 8 mm bead, a 3 mm flat spacer, and a 6 mm color C bicone. Repeat the pattern with color D and E bicones next to the 3 mm flat spacers **(photo 2)**.

3. Repeat the pattern in step 2 until you've covered half the coils. String the flower dangle **(photo 3)**. Repeat the pattern in step 2 until you've covered the remaining coils. Trim the excess memory wire to ⅜ in. (1 cm), and make a loop on the end.

materials

bracelet
- 40 mm stacked Lucite rose
- **19–25** 8 mm round Czech fire-polished beads
- **58–75** 6 mm bicone crystals
    - **20–25** color A
    - **10–13** color B
    - **10–13** color C
    - **9–12** color D
    - **9–12** color E
- **80–100** 4 mm spacers
- **40–50** 3 mm flat spacers
- 2-in. (5 cm) head pin
- memory wire, bracelet diameter

Stacked Lucite rose from The Hole Bead Shop, theholebeadshop.com.

tools & supplies
- Stringing Toolbox, p. 89
- heavy-duty wire cutters or memory-wire cutters

techniques
- stringing
- wirework

DVD review ▶
- Wirework: Plain Loop, Wrapped Loop

Design option

Ring tones. String seed beads on ring-sized memory wire, and showcase a cluster of Lucite flowers. You may want to make the loops at the top of the ring so they don't catch on anything when you're wearing it.

For easy assembly, set aside one repeat of your pattern to refer to while you string.

Fancy findings

Kelsey Lawler knows when you've got pretty components that are jump-ring ready, it doesn't take much to whip up something sensational. Add a few flat-back crystals, attach the dangles, and you've got a tinkling, twinkling set that's easy on the eyes — and your time.

materials

necklace 16–18 in. (41–46 cm)

- **3** 35 mm patinated pendants
- **3** 21 mm patinated bow charms
- **8** 25–30 mm assorted patinated charms
- 6 mm fire-polished bead
- **3–5** 4 mm flat-back crystals
- **18** 3 mm flat-back crystals
- 16–18 in. (41–46 cm) chain, 8–9 mm links
- 1-in. (2.5 cm) head pin
- **14** 6 mm jump rings
- lobster claw clasp

Flat-back crystals from Artbeads.com

tools & supplies

- Stringing Toolbox, p. 89
- Dazzle-Tac jewelry glue
- Hobby Pal pick-up tool

techniques

- stringing

DVD review ▶

- Stringing: Opening and Closing Jump Rings
- Wirework: Wrapped Loop

1. Apply a dot of glue to the center of a pendant, and set a 4 mm flat-back crystal into the glue. Repeat to set six 3 mm flat-backs around the perimeter of the pendant **(photo 1)**. Press the flat-backs, and allow to dry. Make three embellished pendants.

2. Open a 6 mm jump ring (Stringing Basics, p. 89). Attach a bow charm and a pendant, and close the jump ring. Cut a 16–18-in. (41–46 cm) piece of chain. Use a jump ring to attach the dangle to the center link **(photo 2)**.

To set the flat-back crystals, try picking them up with tweezers, a wax stick, a Hobby Pal, or even chainnose pliers. As for the glue: A little goes a long way.

4. On one end of the chain, use a jump ring to attach a lobster claw clasp.

5. On a head pin, string a 6 mm fire-polished bead, and make the first half of a wrapped loop (Wirework Basics, p. 91). Attach the other end link of chain, and complete the wraps.

3. On each side of the dangle, use jump rings to attach a pendant or charm to every other link, ending with a single jump ring attaching two charms.

If you can't find components in colors you like, purchase plain findings and experiment with adding color using the metal patinas and coatings now available.

Design *option*

Easy, breezy earrings. Since these charms are earring-finding friendly, just embellish with flat-backs, and voilà!

Merry-go-round

Get the look of a multistrand necklace without fussing to keep all the strands in their proper place. To achieve the style without the stress, **Kelsey Lawler** strung beads on a continuous strand. To wear: Wrap the strand around and around, and keep the color-blocked sections in place with a ribbon bow.

4. To wear, wrap the strand around your neck five times, and drape as desired. Tie a bow around the strands with a ribbon to keep them in place.

3. To finish: On one end, string a crimp bead. On the other end, string a crimp bead and a large-hole pearl. String each wire end through the crimp beads and large-hole pearl in opposite directions. Tighten the wire, and crimp the crimp beads (Stringing Basics, p. 89). Trim the excess wire.

Necklace
1. Keeping the beading wire on the spool, string an alternating pattern of a pearl and an 11° seed bead until you have strung the entire strand of pearls in that color.

2. Repeat step 1 on the same wire, stringing five strands of pearls, each in a different color. Each section will be 20–21 in. (51–53 cm) in length.

Design *option*

Knot it. Bows not your thing? Knot the strands for a modern twist, or wear them in three long loops for swingy style reminiscent of jewelry from the 1920s.

Substitute a 1¼-in.(3.2 cm) wire for the eye pin in the earring directions and make a plain loop on one end (Wirework Basics, p. 91).

2. On an eye pin, string a pearl and a 3 mm bicone crystal, and make a wrapped loop. Open the loop of the eye pin (Stringing Basics, p. 89), and attach the head pin unit. Close the loop.

3. Open the loop of an earring finding, and attach the dangle. Close the loop.

Earrings

1. For each earring: On a head pin, string a pearl, and make a wrapped loop (Wirework Basics, p. 91).

---

materials

necklace 105 in. (2.5 m)
- **5** 16-in. (41 cm) strands 5 7 mm pearls, assorted colors
- 5–6 g 11º seed beads
- 8 mm large-hole pearl
- flexible beading wire, .014 or .015
- **2** crimp beads
- 12 in. (30 cm) 22 mm ribbon

pair of earrings
- **4** 5–7 mm pearls, **2** in each of **2** colors
- **2** 3 mm bicone crystals
- **2** 1½-in. (3.8 cm) eye pins
- **2** 1½-in. (3.8 cm) head pins
- pair of earring findings

tools & supplies
- Stringing Toolbox, p. 89

techniques
- stringing
- wirework

DVD review ▶
- Stringing: Crimping, Opening and Closing Jump Rings
- Wirework: Wrapped Loop

Pearl on a wire

Melanie Hazen designed this pretty wire frame to showcase favorite beads in her stash. The simple design of this wire perch is easily adapted to a pendant or ring — and it's so budget-friendly, you'll want to make a full set.

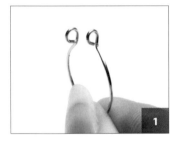

For a punch of color, substitute bright glass or gemstone beads for the pearls.

1. Cut a 2½-in. (6.4 cm) piece of 20-gauge wire, and make a plain loop (Wirework Basics, p. 91) at each end. Shape the wire around a dowel or a ring mandrel at the size 1½ mark.

2. Using chainnose pliers, bend the plain loops so they are parallel to each other **(photo 1)**.

3. On a head pin, string a 3 mm silver bead, a plain loop, a 5 mm pearl, the other plain loop, and a 3 mm. Holding the beads tight against the head pin, make a right-angle bend in the head pin against the last 3 mm **(photo 2)**.

4. Use chainnose pliers to tightly wrap the head pin tail around the wire ring several times. Trim the head pin tail as close to the wraps as possible, and press it against the wire ring **(photo 3)**.

5. Open the loop of an earring finding (Stringing Basics, p. 89), attach the wire frame, and close the loop.

6. Make a second earring.

materials

pair of earrings
- 5 in. (13 cm) 20-gauge wire, dead-soft
- 2 2-in. (5 cm) 24-gauge head pins
- 2 5 mm button pearls
- 4 3 mm round silver beads
- pair of earring findings

tools & supplies
- Wirework Toolbox, p. 91
- ½-in. (1.3 cm) diameter dowel or ring mandrel

technique
- Wirework

DVD review ▶
- Stringing: Opening and Closing Jump Rings
- Wirework: Plain Loop

Design *option*

Make it a set. To make a fun pendant, use heavier gauge wire, increase the length of wire cut in step 1, and use larger beads. Do the same to make a unique ring, forming it to the correct size for your finger.

Tailored Classic

Classic shapes and materials form jewelry that's fashionably on trend yet traditional enough to last, whether it's for a day in the office or a night at the theater. Bright silver and gold metal accents, jewel-toned gemstones and crystals, and traditional shapes and cuts define the jewelry in this section. You'll experiment with stitching small components, try metal clay to make silver earrings, or practice wire-wrapping a lovely herringbone-edged bead frame as you embark on making jewelry for your more tailored days.

Designer doppelganger

For this necklace, **Stacy Werkheiser** made her own connectors with gold-colored seed beads and peyote stitch for a tailored, custom look. The beauty of this over-the-head design is that any gemstone in any shape can be paired with seed beads in whatever metallic hue shows off the stones best.

materials

necklace 30 in. (76 cm)
- **15** 16–18 mm gemstone beads (green crackle agate)
- 2 g 8º seed beads (Miyuki 2, silver-lined light gold)
- 8 g 11º seed beads (Miyuki 4, silver-lined dark gold)
- 5 g 15º seed beads (Miyuki 3, silver-lined gold)
- 8 ft. (2.4 m) 22-gauge wire
- **22** 7 mm oval jump rings
- Fireline 6 lb. test

tools & supplies
- Stitching Toolbox, p. 89
- Wirework Toolbox, p. 91

techniques
- peyote stitch
- wirework

DVD review
- Stringing: Opening and Closing Jump Rings
- Wireworking: Wrapped Loop
- Stitching: Ending and Adding Thread, Overhand Knot, Peyote Stitch–Joining Ends, Tubular Peyote Stitch

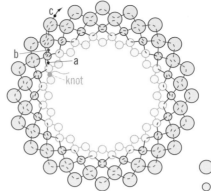

figure

○ 11º seed bead
○ 15º seed bead

Design *option*

Earrings, anyone? Adapt the "Gemstone units" to make earrings: Cut a 6-in. (15 cm) piece of 22-gauge wire, and make a wrapped loop on one end. String a bead, leaving a little space between the top of the bead and the bottom of the wraps. Wrap the remaining wire around the bead and below the wrapped loop. Trim the excess wire, and attach an earring finding.

Peyote connectors

1. On 1½ yd. (1.4 m) of Fireline, center 40 15ºs seed beads. Tie the beads into a ring with a square knot (Stitching Basics, p. 89). With one end of thread, sew through the next 15º.

2. With this thread, work one round of tubular peyote stitch (Stitching Basics) with 15ºs **(figure, a–b)**, then work two rounds with 11º seed beads **(b–c)**. Do not end the thread.

3. Switch to the other thread, and make sure it is exiting a 15º up-bead in the first round. Work two rounds of tubular peyote with 15ºs and three rounds with 11ºs. Zip up (Stitching Basics) the edges of the beadwork, and end this thread (Stitching Basics).

4. With the remaining end of thread, exit an 11º up-bead in the outer round of 11ºs. Work a peyote stitch with an 8º seed bead, and sew through the next two 11ºs, exiting the next 11º in the outer round **(photo 1)**. Repeat to complete the round, then sew through the beadwork to exit the first 8º added.

5. Pick up nine 15ºs, and sew through the 8º again in the same direction, forming a loop above the 8º **(photo 2)**. Retrace the thread path through the loop, and sew through the 8º again.

6. Sew through the beadwork to exit the 8º on the opposite side of the peyote connector, and repeat step 5. Sew into the beadwork, and end the thread.

7. Make a total of seven peyote connectors.

Gemstone units

1. Cut a 4-in. (10 cm) piece of 22-gauge wire, and make a wrapped loop (Wirework Basics, p. 91) on one end. String a gemstone bead, and make a wrapped loop.

2. Repeat step 1 to make a total of nine gemstone units.

3. Cut a 10-in. (25 cm) piece of wire, and make a wrapped loop on one end. String a gemstone bead, and make a wrapped loop, but do not cover the entire wire stem with the wraps **(photo 3)**.

4. Hold the bead against the wrapped loop just made, and wrap the remaining wire around the bead several times. Wrap the end of the wire below the wraps of the first wrapped loop **(photo 4)**. Trim the excess wire.

5. Repeat steps 3 and 4 to make a total of six wire-wrapped gemstone units.

Assembly

Use 7 mm oval jump rings (Stringing Basics, p. 89) to connect the components.

Multistrands mastered

4. On each end of each strand, string a 6 mm and four or five 15º seed beads. Check the fit, and add or remove beads if necessary. (see Sidebar, p. 25). On each end, over all three strands, string a teardrop and a crimp bead.

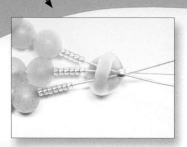

5. On each end, over all three strands, string half of the clasp. Go back through the crimp beads, tighten the wire, and crimp the crimp beads (Stringing Basics). Trim the excess wire.

Necklace

1. For the shortest strand, cut a piece of beading wire (Stringing Basics, p. 89). String an alternating pattern of 6 mm round beads and 13 mm teardrop beads until the strand is within 2 in. (5 cm) of the finished length. My inner strand is 17 in. (43 cm).

2. For the middle strand, cut a piece of beading wire 3 in. (7.6 cm) longer than the first. String a 5-in. (13 cm) section of 6 mms and teardrops. String a 22 mm Venetian bead, then string 6 mms and teardrops until the strand is within 2 in. (5 cm) of the finished length. My middle strand is 20 in. (51 cm).

3. For the longest strand, cut a piece of beading wire 2 in. (5 cm) longer than the previous piece. String an alternating pattern of 6 mms and teardrops until the strand is within 2 in. (5 cm) of the finished length. My longest strand is 22 in. (56 cm).

Follow **Cathy Jakicic's** advice: Whether you're going for a meticulously paced or a clustered look, a three-strand necklace is rarely put together 1-2-3. Be prepared to check the drape and fit several times and add or remove beads until it's perfect. When measuring the strands of teardrop beads, make sure the round beads are nestled in the teardrops before you finish the necklace or you'll end up with unwanted slack.

Drop in price. The beauty of three lampworked teardrop strands comes at an impressive price tag. These 6 mm fire-polished drops are a more budget-friendly option.

2. Use a 5 mm jump ring to attach the teardrop dangle and an earring finding.

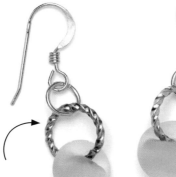

Earrings

1. For each earring: Open a 10 mm decorative jump ring (Stringing Basics, p. 89), and attach a teardrop bead. Close the jump ring.

materials

necklace 17–21 in. (43–53 cm)
- 22 mm Venetian disk bead
- **130–140** 13 mm lampworked teardrop beads
- **130–140** 6 mm round beads
- 1 g 15º seed beads
- flexible beading wire, .014 or .015
- **2** crimp beads
- toggle clasp

pair of earrings
- **2** 13 mm lampworked teardrop beads
- **2** 10 mm decorative jump rings
- **2** 5 mm jump rings
- pair of earring findings

Venetian beads from Bella Venetian Beads, bellavenetianbeads.com. Teardrop beads from Unicorne Beads, (714) 572-8558, unicornebeads.com.

tools & supplies
- Stringing Toolbox, p. 89

techniques
- Stringing

DVD review ▶
- Stringing: Crimping, Opening and Closing Jump Rings

It's all about measuring

- Start by making each strand one or two inches longer than the last. Use a bead board to organize the strands.
- Check the drape by holding the strands around your neck. Ideally, attach the strands to the clasp, temporarily securing them with tape or Bead Stoppers. You can also estimate the extra length the clasp will add.
- Add or remove beads until you achieve the desired results. Make big changes by adding or removing teardrops and rounds, or make tiny adjustments with seed beads.
- Repeat the process as needed. Be prepared to do this several times — it's worth the trouble to get the most flattering drape.

BEAD DESIGN BOARD

Stamping in style

Jill L. Erickson makes a pair of double-sided earrings with just two pinches of metal clay. Jill attributes the technique to a tip from Gail Crosman Moore: Aligned back to back, matched pairs of stampings make wonderful metal clay molds. These Art Nouveau-style drops hang from handmade earring findings.

Design *option*

Matching game. Use larger stampings to make a pendant to match or coordinate with your earrings.

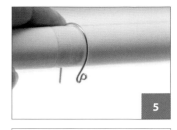

Earring dangle components

1. Select a matched pair of brass stampings that fit together when aligned back to back. To conserve clay and make lightweight earrings, choose stamps with fairly shallow depressions. Use flush cutters to snip off loops from the stampings if they have them, and smooth the cut edges with a flat needle file.

2. Using a sponge applicator or flat-tip paintbrush, apply a thin coat of olive oil or hand balm to the recessed side of the stampings.

3. Remove about 4 g of metal clay from its package, and seal the unused clay to keep it hydrated. Pinch the clay into roughly the shape of your stamp. Sandwich the clay and one embeddable jump ring between the brass stampings. Squeeze the stampings so that their edges meet. Excess clay will be forced outside the mold **(photo 1)**. Use your fingers to peel away the excess clay, and seal it back in the package for future use. Check that the jump ring is aligned properly, and adjust the jump ring's position as necessary.

4. While the clay is wet, use your fingernail to gently pry the top stamping from the clay. Then, carefully peel the clay component from the remaining stamping, holding the component by its edges.

5. Place the semi-dry component on a mug warmer to dry completely. Flip the component over every few minutes so that it dries evenly; this minimizes the occurrence of curled edges.

6. Support the completely dry component on a rubber block, and use needle files or your favorite sanding tools to smooth and refine the edges of the component **(photo 2)**.

7. Repeat steps 1–6 to make a second component.

Firing and finishing

1. Place one component on a firing brick, and fire with a handheld butane torch **(photo 3** and Clays and Resin Basics, p. 92) according to the clay manufacturer's instructions. Use metal tweezers to quench the component in water. Repeat to fire and quench the second component.

2. Use a soft brass brush and soapy water to polish and work-harden the components, then rinse them in clean water. Alternatively, use a tumbler with steel shot and burnishing compound to polish the components.

3. If desired, add patina to the components: String a piece of scrap wire through each component's jump ring, and dip them into a solution of liver of sulfur **(photo 4** and Metalwork Basics, p. 92).

Rinse the components with water, and dry them with a soft cloth. Use 0000 steel wool to remove patina from the high points.

Earring findings

1. Using flush cutters, cut two 2½-in. (6.4 cm) pieces of 20-gauge wire. With a planishing hammer and a bench block or anvil, flatten one end of each wire.

2. With roundnose pliers, grasp the flattened end of a wire, and make a small loop. At the base of the loop, bend the wire back in the opposite direction until it almost touches the first loop. Repeat to bend the second wire.

3. Using your fingers, bend a wire around the barrel of a thick dowel or marker **(photo 5)**. Repeat to bend the second wire.

4. Use a cup bur or wire rounder to smooth the ends of the earring findings. Slide an earring component onto each finding.

materials

pair of earrings
- 6–10 g metal clay (fine silver)
- 5 in. (13 cm) 20-gauge round sterling silver or Argentium sterling silver wire
- pair of matched brass stampings
- **2** 3 mm embeddable fine-silver jump rings

Embeddable jump rings from Metal Clay Findings, metalclayfindings.com. Brass stampings from Gail Crosman Moore, gailcrosmanmoore.com.

tools & supplies
- Wirework Toolbox, p. 91
- Clays and Resin Toolbox, p. 92
- tumbler with steel shot and burnishing compound (optional)
- 0000 steel wool (optional)
- planishing hammer
- mug warmer
- glass sheet
- rubber block
- metal tweezers
- dowel or marker

techniques
- metal clay
- wirework

DVD review ▶
- Clays and Resins: Torch-Firing Metal Clay

Diamond leaf necklace

Fashion in a flash

Divine rock necklace

Rectangles and dangles necklace

Sew-on stones are usually flat-back, two-hole rhinestones (drilled front to back) that are intended for sewing on fabric. **Diane Fitzgerald** sees the endless possibilities for jewelry design offered by the variety of shapes, colors, and foiling in these adornments. With a few readily available parts, she's created sophisticated necklaces, bracelets, and even earrings that are still quick and easy to make.

Multiply the glamour. Make a bold fashion statement with a three-strand bracelet. Each strand of this bracelet contains 11 12 x 6 mm navette stones connected by 8 mm diamond clips.

Design *option*

I used two types of connectors for the jewelry shown: pinch bails, sometimes known as "ice pick bails," and chandelier parts.

You need only the most basic tools for assembling these gorgeous pieces: roundnose pliers, chainnose or flatnose pliers, and wire cutters. When bending the connector legs around the hole of a stone, be sure to allow room between the tip of the pliers and the stone to prevent chipping. Work slowly.

As with any foil-backed stone or crystal, take care when storing or packing them to prevent the metal connectors from scratching the foil. I usually place the piece flat on bubble wrap, then roll up the bubble wrap.

Pinch bails

Pinch bails are stamped metal parts shaped to resemble pincers with a ring at the top. For these projects, the prongs of a pinch bail are inserted into the hole of a sew-on stone,

then the sides of the bail are pinched together with chainnose or flatnose pliers **(photo 1)**. Each pinch bail is then connected to the next one with a jump ring **(photo 2)**.

Chandelier parts

Chandelier parts resemble staples used to connect sheets of paper. In chandelier language, they are referred to as hangers because they are used to hang crystals from chandeliers. The following

instructions refer to them as connectors. They may be gold or chrome plated and are available with the front or exposed part in the shape of a bow tie, an elongated triangle, or a simple narrow diamond. They range in size from 8 mm to 17 mm. The "legs" of these connectors are usually about 8 mm in length but they are also available with extra-long legs (16 mm).

To connect two stones using chandelier parts, insert one of the connector legs into

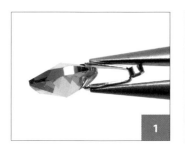

Navette necklace

Square/oval/ cosmic necklace

Fun fact

Sew-on stones are a type of rhinestone, a term that today refers to glass, crystal, or acrylic stones made to simulate diamonds. Originally, rhinestones were rock crystals gathered from the river Rhine.

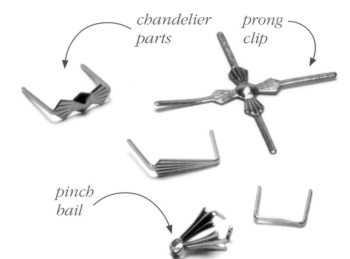

chandelier parts

prong clip

pinch bail

Design *option*

Instant style. To make super-easy earrings, attach a pinch bail to a top-drilled pendant, and attach the loop of the bail to an earring finding.

---

a hole of a sew-on stone with the front of the connector aligned with the front of the stone **(photo 3)**.

Holding the stone in one hand, grab the tip of the leg with pliers, and bend the leg toward the back of the connector **(photo 4)**. To be sure the tip of the leg is touching the back of the connector, you may have to squeeze it gently with chainnose or flatnose pliers. Be sure the sew-on stone moves freely in the connector loop. Attach another stone to the other leg of the connector.

In some cases, the legs may be too long and you may need to shorten them by clipping off about 1–2 mm with wire cutters.

materials

diamond leaf necklace 17½ in. (44.5 cm)
- **17** 10 x 9 mm diamond leaf sew-on stones (Art. 3254, olivine)
- **18** 12 mm brass hangers (goldtone)
- clasp

divine rock necklace 16½ in. (41.9 cm)
- **15** 19 x 13 mm divine rock sew-on stones (Art. 3257, red magma)
- **16** 12 mm brass hangers (goldtone)
- clasp

rectangles and dangles necklace 16 in. (41 cm)
- **15** 18 x 13 mm rectangle sew-on stones (Art. 3250, jet hematite)
- **16** 12 x 4 mm metal drops (goldtone)
- **16** 11 mm 4-prong clips

with top prong of each clipped off and filed (goldtone)
- clasp

navette necklace 16½ in. (41.9 cm)
- **12** 12 x 6 mm navette sew-on stones (Art. 3223, jet)
- **11** 12 x 6 mm navette sew-on stones (Art. 3223, metallic light-gold foiled)
- **24** 10.5 mm brass bow-tie hangers (goldtone)
- clasp

square/oval/cosmic necklace 17 in. (43 cm)
- **4** 22 mm square sew-on stones (Art. 3240, crystal dorado)
- **2** 26 x 21 mm cosmic sew-on stones (Art. 3265, crystal golden shadow)
- **3** 24 x 17 mm oval sew-on

stones (Art. 3210, crystal copper)
- **2** 14 mm rivoli sew-on stones (Art. 3200, jet nut)
- **22** 8 x 3 mm pinch bails (goldtone darkened with liver of sulfur)
- **12** 4 mm jump rings
- clasp

All sew-on stones by Swarovski Elements. Pinch bails available at firemountaingems.com and riogrande.com. Brass hangers from chandelierparts.com. Check local bead stores for all other supplies.

tools & supplies
- Stringing Toolbox, p. 89

techniques
- stringing

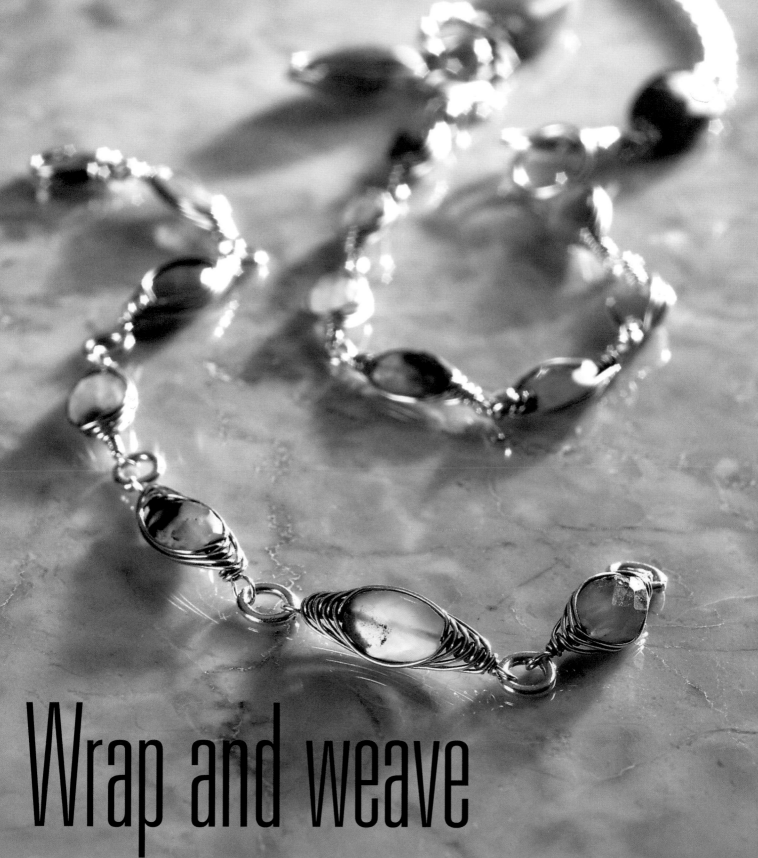

Wrap and weave

Kris Silva used this clever technique to frame beads with a stunning herringbone wire-woven pattern. It's a simple way to elevate the look of any bead strand. You could even try it with found objects that are similar in size and shape. To experiment with the drama level, adjust the number of times you weave around each bead when you make the bezel.

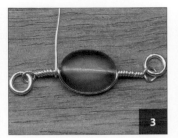
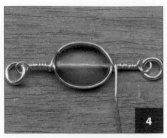

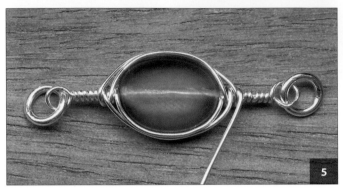

1. Cut a 12-in. (30 cm) piece of 24-gauge (0.51 mm) wire. To straighten the wire, grasp one end with chainnose pliers, and pull the wire through nylon-jaw pliers.

2. On one end of the wire, make the first half of a wrapped loop (Wirework Basics, p. 91). Slide the 10 mm soldered jump ring into the loop, and complete the wraps, making six to eight wraps **(photo 1)**.

3. To measure the length of the wraps so you can make them consistent for each component, lay the chainnose pliers along the wraps, positioning the tips of the jaws near the loop. Use painter's tape or a pen to mark the jaw where the wraps end.

4. String a 6 mm bead on the wire. With the tips of the chainnose pliers touching the bead, align the pliers along the bare wire. At the point on the wire that aligns with the mark on the pliers, make the first half of a wrapped loop in the same plane as the first loop.

5. Slide a 3 mm soldered jump ring into the loop, and complete the wraps until you reach the bead. Do not cut the wire **(photo 2)**.

6. Bring the wire along one side of the bead, then make one wrap next to the bead, wrapping around the core wire **(photo 3)**. Repeat on the other side of the bead **(photo 4)**. Continue **(photo 5)** until you reach the component's loops. Make two more wraps around

the core wire, trim the excess wrapping wire, and tuck the tail into the wraps **(photo 6)**.

7. Work as in steps 1 and 2 to make the next component, but instead of attaching a 10 mm soldered jump ring, attach the 3 mm ring from the previous component. Repeat steps 3–6 to complete the component.

8. Make six components for a 7½-in. (19.1 cm) bracelet. When making the last component, attach a lobster claw clasp instead of a soldered jump ring to the last loop.

materials

bracelet 7½ in. (19.1 cm)
- **6** 6 mm beads
- **6** ft. (1.8 m) 24-gauge (0.51 mm) wire, dead-soft
- **6** 3 mm soldered jump rings
- lobster claw clasp and 10 mm soldered jump ring

tools & supplies
- Wirework Toolbox, p. 91
- painter's tape or pen (optional)

techniques
- wirework

DVD review ▶
- Wirework: Wrapped Loop

Short on soldered jump rings? Attach single links of chain instead.

Tips on wrapping wire

For each time you plan to go around a bead to make the herringbone pattern, you need two wire wraps on the core wire. This means that six wraps will allow for three times around a bead, and eight wraps will allow for four times around a bead.

If you want a denser herringbone frame with more wire paths surrounding a bead, make additional wraps around the core wire, keeping the number of wraps even. You may need more than 12 in. (30 cm) of wire to make each component, depending on the size of the bead and how many wraps you want.

It's easier to make wraps when you hold the core wire firmly. After you've made three wraps, reposition your pliers to grasp the wraps rather than the loop. Gripping the wraps gives you more leverage and control, and so subsequent wraps are easier to form.

Design *option*

Make it a choker. It's easy to turn this bracelet into a choker — all you need is a simple extender. Here, two bead units are connected with chain. A lobster claw clasp is attached to one end of the extender and a soldered jump ring to the other. A dangle, woven with the herringbone pattern, is attached to the extender's soldered jump ring. To connect the extender and the bracelet, just attach the lobster claw clasps to the soldered jump rings, and you're done!

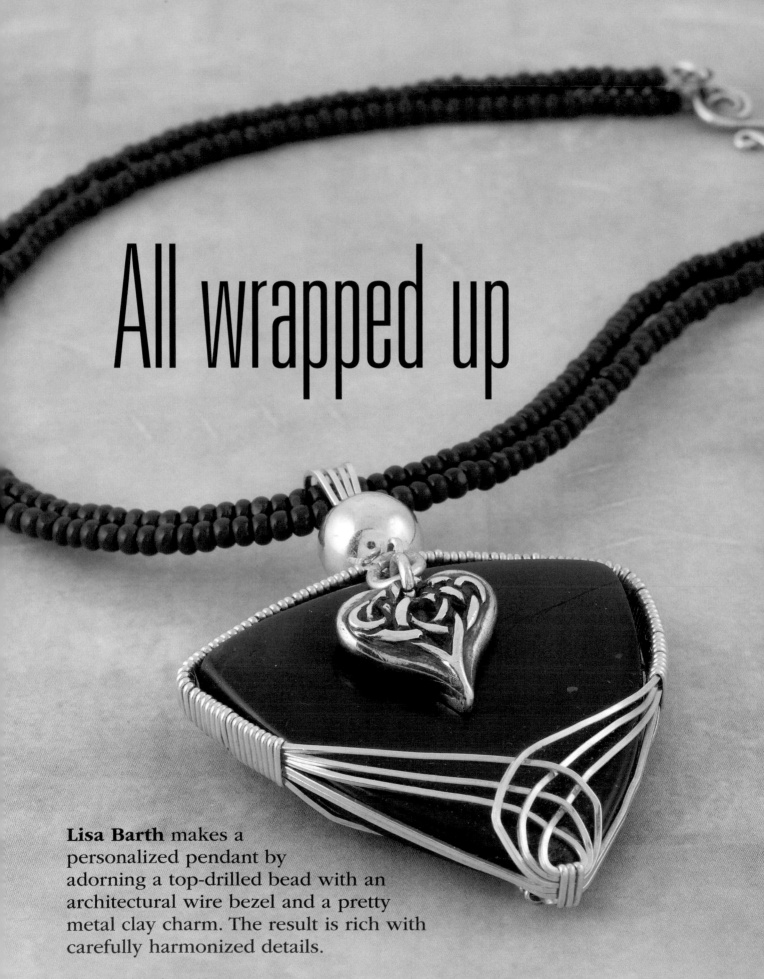

All wrapped up

Lisa Barth makes a personalized pendant by adorning a top-drilled bead with an architectural wire bezel and a pretty metal clay charm. The result is rich with carefully harmonized details.

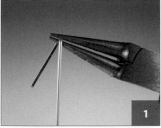

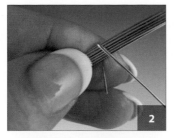

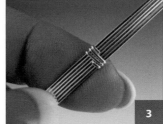

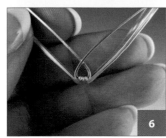

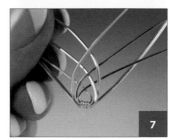

Wire-wrapped pendant

1. Calculate the perimeter of your stone by wrapping a string around the edge and marking where it crosses itself. Measure the length of the string, add 3 in. (7.6 cm) to that number, and cut six pieces of 22-gauge square wire to that length. (For this stone, the perimeter was 5¼ in./13.3 cm. Adding 3 in./7.6 cm brought the length to 8¼ in./21 cm for each of the six square wires.)

2. Cut two 18-in. (46 cm) pieces of 22-gauge half-round wire. These are your wrapping wires. Cut one 4-in. (10 cm) piece of half-round wire. Using roundnose pliers, make a sharp bend in the 4-in. (10 cm) wire ½ in. (1.3 cm) from one end **(photo 1).**

> *Check your wirework against the shape of the stone frequently as you work to ensure the best fit for your pendant.*

3. Stack the six pieces of square wire on top of each other to form a flat row. Hook the bend in the 4-in. (10 cm) half-round wire over the middle of the six square wires **(photo 2)**. Wrap the 4-in. (10 cm) wire tightly around the six square wires three times. Trim the ends of the 4-in. (10 cm) wire so they fall in the middle of the back side of the six wires. Using flatnose pliers, pinch the wraps tightly over the square wires. This should lock the wraps in place so they do not slide **(photo 3)**.

4. Using chainnose pliers, grasp the wraps tightly, and bend the square wires upward so they form a large V **(photo 4)**. Make sure the V is the appropriate angle for the point of the stone **(photo 5)**.

> *If you prefer, use a pre-made charm instead of making one with metal clay.*

5. Holding the wires horizontal with the ends of the wraps facing away from you, gently pull the top wire from the right side over to the left side and the top wire from the left side over to the right side **(photo 6)**. Repeat with the second set of wires, crossing them over the first wires, and again with the third set of wires **(photo 7)**.

6. Flip your work over so you can access the last pair of square wires. Using flatnose pliers, grasp the last square wire on the right, and bend it down toward the middle. Repeat with the last wire on the left. Bend each wire back out about ½ in. (1.3 cm) from the half-round wire wraps **(photo 8)**.

materials
pendant 1¾ x 2¼ in. (4.4 x 5.7 cm)
- 40 mm top-drilled triangular stone pendant
- 10 mm bead with 4 mm hole
- 10 g fine-silver metal clay
- 1½ yd. (1.4 m) 22-gauge square wire, half-hard
- 44 in. (1.1 m) 22-gauge half-round wire, half-hard
- **2** 3 mm jump rings

tools & supplies
- Wirework Toolbox, p. 91
- Clays and Resin Toolbox, p. 92
- Metalwork Toolbox, p. 92
- stepped pliers
- mold or texture plate
- food dehydrator (optional)
- rubber block
- square jeweler's file
- metal tweezers

techniques
- wirework
- metal clay

DVD review ▶
- Metalwork: Adding Patina with Liver of Sulfur
- Stringing: Opening and Closing Jump Rings
- Clays and Resin: Rolling and Cutting Metal Clay, Torch-Firing Metal Clay

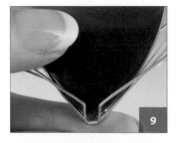

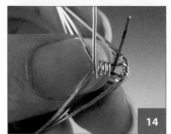

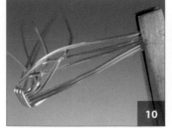

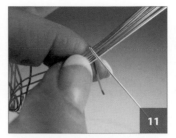

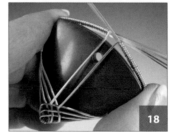

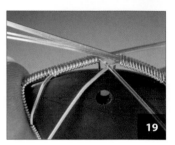

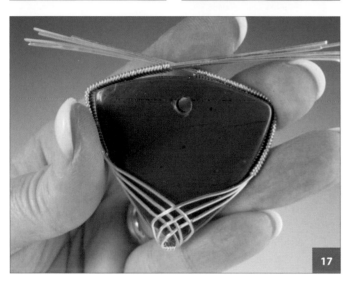

7. Position the stone in the bezel between the crisscross in the front and the two bent wires on the back **(photo 9)**. It may be a tight fit. Remove the stone.

8. Using flatnose pliers, pinch together the six square wires on one side of the frame, keeping them stacked as in step 3 **(photo 10)**. The closer you stack the wires together, the easier it will be to get a tight frame.

9. Using roundnose pliers, make a sharp bend ½ in. (1.3 cm) from the end of one 18-in. (46 cm) wrapping wire.

Hook the wrapping wire around the six square wires on the side. Hold the tail of the wrapping wire tightly against the square wires with your index finger as you begin to wrap **(photo 11)**. This will stabilize the wire and help you start out wrapping tightly. Wrap the wire around the six square wires eight times.

10. Bend the sixth square wire (counting from the front of the frame) toward the other side of the pendant **(photo 12)**. Continue wrapping around the five remaining square wires six more times **(photo 13)**.

11. Pinch together the remaining six square wires, making the sides of the frame as symmetrical as possible. Make a hook ½ in. (1.3 cm) from the end of the remaining wrapping wire, and hook the six square wires. Wrap four times, as in step 9, then pause to measure the distance from the point of the V to the wraps, and compare to the other side. Slide the wraps as needed to make the frame symmetrical, and check the fit of the stone. Using flatnose pliers, pinch the four wraps tight to the square wires, and wrap four more times. Repeat step 10 on this side.

12. Trim the short ends of the wrapping wires so that the ends fall inside the frame and won't be seen from the front. Gently pinch them into place. Do not cut the long ends of the wrapping wires.

13. Cut a 4-in. (10 cm) piece of 22-gauge half-round wire, and make a hook ½ in. (1.3 cm) from one end. Hook the wire around the two square wires at the back of the frame that you bent in step 6. Carefully wrap around the two wires three times **(photo 14)**, then trim the wrapping wire so the ends fall inside the frame.

14. Continue wrapping the five square wires on one side until you have a total of 22 wraps. Fit the stone inside the frame. Once you have a good fit, bend the side around the corner of the stone **(photo 15)**. Make sure it conforms to the shape of the stone. Remove the stone.

15. Fit the sixth square wire back into the group, and wrap around the six square wires four more times **(photo 16)**. Pinch these wraps tightly around the six square wires.

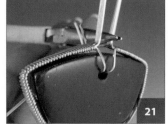

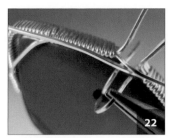

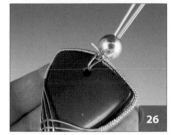

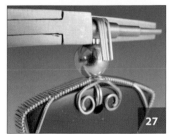

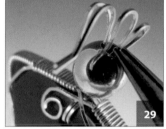

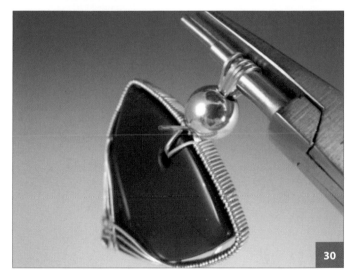

16. Repeat steps 14 and 15 on the other side. Continue to wrap both sides until they almost meet in the middle, keeping them symmetrical. Trim the wrapping wires so the ends fall inside the frame. Fit the stone in the frame (**photo 17**).

17. On each side, bend the first square wire straight down against the front of the stone (**photo 18**). On the back, cross the sixth square wires above the hole in the stone (**photo 19**).

18. From the front, feed the first set of square wires through the hole in the stone, pulling them tight against the front (**photo 20**). This should pull the wrapped portion of the frame tight against the edges of the stone.

19. Using chainnose pliers, bend the remaining four square wires on each side of the frame straight up (**photo 21**).

20. Using chainnose pliers, grasp the two wires coming out of the hole, and tuck them under the crossed square wires on the back of the frame (**photo 22**). Trim one of the wires from the hole so that the end will be hidden on top of the frame between the two sets of remaining square wires (**photo 23**). The other wire should stick straight out in the front, and will be used later to hang the charm.

21. On the back of the frame, trim both of the crossed square wires so they are about 1 in. (2.5 cm) long. Use roundnose

pliers to curl each end into a swirl (**photo 24**).

22. Trim the outside square wires on each side so they are ¼ in. (6 mm) long (**photo 25**).

23. Slide the 10 mm bead onto the remaining four square wires. Tuck the four ¼-in. (6 mm) wires inside the bead (**photo 26**).

24. Using stepped pliers, pinch together the four square wires above the bead, curve the wires over the pliers, and trim

to the same length, near the center of the 10 mm bead (**photo 27**).

25. Using chainnose pliers, make a bend near the end of all four square wires (**photo 28**). This bend will form a lip that will catch the inside edge of the bead and make a sturdy bail that will not easily pull out. Working with one wire at a time, fit the end of each wire into the 10 mm bead (**photo 29**). Use the stepped pliers to gently shape the bail loop (**photo 30**).

31

32

33

34

26. Using roundnose pliers, make a small loop in the remaining wire on the front of the pendant **(photo 31)**.

Metal clay charm

1. Knead 10 grams of metal clay with your fingers by folding it in half three or four times. This warms it up and conditions it a bit, getting it ready to use.

2. Roll out the metal clay (Clays and Resin Basics, p. 93) on a nonstick surface, using a 3 mm rolling guide or two stacks of three playing cards.

3. Place the metal clay on the mold or texture plate of your choice. Gently push down with the tips of your fingers, ensuring that the metal clay has full contact with the mold or texture plate **(photo 32)**.

4. Using a needle tool, cut out the shape you want, leaving a little room on the edges for refining **(photo 33)**.

5. Let the charm dry completely. This can take 24 hours to air-dry, or you can speed up the process by placing the piece in a food dehydrator dedicated to metal clay.

6. When the piece is dry, place it on a rubber block, and refine the edges and back with a sanding sponge and needle file.

In order to torch-fire the charm, it should be smaller than a U.S. silver dollar.

7. Using a square jeweler's file, slowly and gently drill out a hole at the top of the charm by turning the file back and forth **(photo 34)**. Refine the hole so the inside is smooth.

8. Place the dry piece on a firing brick on top of a heat-resistant surface. Fire with a butane torch (Clays and Resin Basics).

9. Pick up the piece with metal tweezers, and quench it in water. Dry with a paper towel.

10. Use a brass brush and soapy water to polish the piece **(photo 35)**. Burnish the piece with an agate burnisher, if desired.

11. If desired, add a patina to the piece with liver of sulfur (Metalwork Basics, p. 92).

12. Buff the surface using a silver polishing cloth.

13. To attach the charm to the pendant, open two jump rings (Stringing Basics, p. 89), and slide the charm on one. Close the jump ring. Use the second jump ring to attach the charm jump ring and the loop on the pendant **(photo 36)**.

35

36

If your piece starts to glow a bright red, remove the heat and let the color dim before you reapply heat and continue timing.

Design *option*

String it up. This pendant looks great on a wide range of necklace bases, including a thick chain, strands of seed beads, or a stitched rope.

Urban Edge

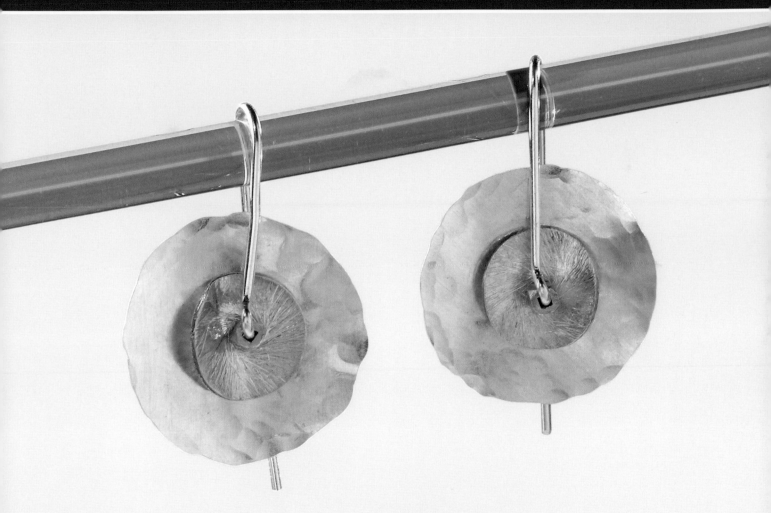

Pair your little black dress with dark tights and over-the-knee boots, and instantly switch your style from daily demure to night-on-the-town wow. The perfect accessory eases the transition, whether it's a necklace that juxtaposes dark metal chain with cool, clear crystal; a sleek bracelet showing two-toned chain mail; or a bold, textural cuff stitched from gray and black peanut beads, pearls, and crystals.

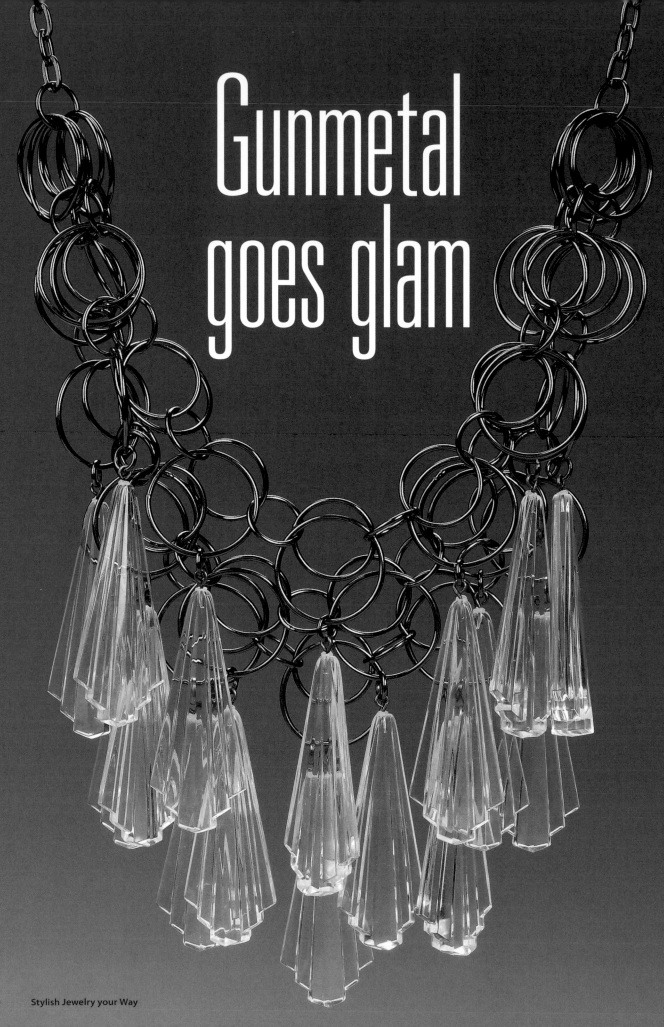

Gunmetal goes glam

You won't need much to create a cascading collar — just some icy Lucite pendants and a length of large-link chain. **Naomi Fujimoto** paired colorless Deco-style pendants with cool gunmetal, but any dramatic drop will do!

Necklace

1. Cut three pieces of double-link chain: 9–10 in. (23–25 cm), 10–12 in. (25–30 cm), and 11–14 in. (28–36 cm).

2. Open a 6 mm jump ring (Stringing Basics, p. 89), and attach a pendant and the 22 mm center link of the shortest chain. Close the jump ring. On each side, use a 6 mm jump ring to attach a pendant for a total of three pendants **(photo 1)**. If the chain has an even number of 22 mm links, attach a total of four pendants.

3. On the medium-length chain, use jump rings to attach six or seven pendants. On the longest chain, use jump rings to attach seven or eight pendants. Check the drape, and trim chain from each end if necessary **(photo 2)**.

4. Cut two 2–4-in. (5–10 cm) pieces of cable chain. Use an 11–13 mm jump ring to attach one end of each double-link chain and a cable chain **(photo 3)**. Repeat on the other end of the double-link chains.

5. Use a 6 mm jump ring to attach a lobster claw clasp and the remaining end of a cable chain. Use a 6 mm jump ring to attach an 11 13 mm jump ring to the other chain.

Earrings

For each earring: Open the loop of an earring finding (Stringing Basics, p. 89), and attach a pendant. Close the loop.

materials

necklace 15 in. (38 cm)
- **16–19** 50 mm Lucite Art Deco pendants
- **32–38** in. (81–97 cm) double-link chain, 22 mm links
- **5–9** in. (13–23 cm) cable chain, 8–10 mm links
- **3** 11–13 mm jump rings
- **18–21** 6 mm jump rings
- lobster claw clasp

pair of earrings
- **2** 50 mm Lucite Art Deco pendants
- pair of earring findings

Lucite pendants and double-link chain from JewelCraft, jewelcraft.biz.

tools & supplies
- Stringing Toolbox, p. 89

techniques
- stringing

DVD review ▶
- Stringing: Opening and Closing Jump Rings

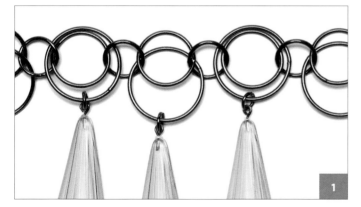

Use budget-friendly cable chain for the back of the necklace; most of it won't be visible when worn.

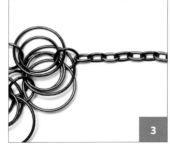

Design *option*

Simply chain.
For a bold, graphic design, make a bracelet with three pieces of chain. Hammer the links for more dimension.

Blow-by-blow bangles

materials

bangle 7½–8½ in. (19.1–21.6 cm)
- 7½–8½ in. (19.1–21.6 cm) 12-gauge (2.03 mm) round fine-silver wire

tools & supplies
- Metalwork Toolbox, p. 92
- heavy-duty flush cutters
- torch station: butane torch, charcoal block, heat-proof surface
- bench anvil (horned)
- bench vise
- metal design stamps
- utility hammer
- liver of sulfur

technique
- metalwork

DVD review ▶
- Metalwork: Adding Patina with Liver of Sulfur

Fun fact

"Work-hardening" means moving metal (by twisting it, pounding it, or shaping it, for example) which compresses the metal's molecules and makes the metal more rigid.

Kim Otterbein uses stamps and a hammer to embellish and work-harden these fine silver bangles. Typically, work-hardening is its own step separate from the fun stuff, but in this project, you use metal design stamps to decorate the soft silver wire as you harden them into a shape that will hold.

1. Using heavy-duty flush cutters, cut a piece of 12-gauge (2.03 mm) fine-silver wire a bit shorter than your desired bracelet circumference (the bangle will expand as you stamp it). I cut mine to 7½ in. (19.1 cm). File the ends flat with a needle file.

2. Curve the wire until the ends meet flush. You may have to bend the ends past each other several times **(photo 1)** so that the ends will stay together without a gap. The wire does not have to be in a perfect circle; you'll shape it after you fuse it.

3. Place your wire on a charcoal block. Heat the wire evenly with a butane torch, but focus on the wire ends, moving the flame across the join **(photo 2)**. When the silver is hot enough to fuse, it will become white and matte-looking. At that point, watch for the silver to turn shiny on both wire ends.

While the wire ends are shiny, move the flame back and forth across the join to guide the molten silver, fusing the wire ends.

To avoid melting the wire, remove the heat as soon as the ends fully fuse. Either let the bangle air-cool or quench it in water.

4. Use your hands to shape the bangle into a circle. Secure a bench anvil in a bench vise. Lay the bangle on the anvil's flat surface.

Holding a metal design stamp against one side of the bangle, hit the stamp with a utility hammer hard enough to make a clear impression in the bangle. Continue stamping around the bangle **(photo 3)**. Flip the bangle over, and stamp the other side.

Don't strike the wire too hard; strike just hard enough to clearly see the stamp's indentation. (This will slightly flatten the impressions on the first side, but if you've hit the stamps hard enough on the first side, both sides should show up well.)

5. Using one hand, hold the bracelet on its edge on the anvil's horn. Use that same hand to rest a stamp on the bangle's outer edge. Strike the stamp with the hammer. Continue stamping around the bangle's edge **(photo 4)**.

6. Add a patina with liver of sulfur (Metalwork Basics, p. 92) until you achieve the desired color for the indentations. Rinse the bangle in water, and use a polishing cloth to buff patina from the high points.

Design *option*

Make multiples. Wearing several of these bangles together will make a multilayered, clinky fashion statement. Before you make multiple bangles, make just one first to serve as a template. Your hammering style will determine how much the wire expands during stamping, so a template bangle will allow you to pinpoint the length of wire you should start out with.

Fashion bound

Anna Elizabeth Draeger mixes and matches a variety of chains and creates a unique closure with small sections of herringbone stitch. The quick-to-stitch tabs at the ends of this bracelet both display and also evenly space the chains.

Sans stitching. To create this fashionable accessory in a flash, skip the stitched tabs, and connect the chains directly to the multistrand clasp. This style also works as a necklace by adjusting the lengths of the chains to drape at any length desired.

1. On 1½ yd. (1.4 m) of Fireline, pick up four 10º cylinder beads, leaving a 15-in. (38 cm) tail. Sew through all four cylinders again, stacking the beads into two columns. Working in ladder stitch (Stitching Basics, p. 89), pick up two cylinders per stitch to make a strip of beadwork two beads tall and 14 stitches long. Zigzag back through the beadwork so the working thread and tail are exiting opposite ends of the first stitch in the strip.

2. Work a row of flat herringbone stitch (Stitching Basics) using two cylinders per stitch. At the end of the row, make a concealed turn (Stitching Basics). Repeat this step for a total of four rows of herringbone stitch.

3. For the next row, pick up two cylinders and a soldered jump ring per stitch, making sure the soldered jump ring sits centered between the two cylinders in each stitch **(photo 1)**. After completing the row, sew through all the beads in the end column, then reinforce the beadwork by zigzagging through the remaining columns. Sew through the beadwork to exit the end bead in the last row added.

4. Work the final row using only one cylinder per stitch; then end the working thread (Stitching Basics).

5. Using the tail, sew through the beadwork to exit a bead in the first herringbone row that corresponds with a clasp loop

(photo 2). Sew through the loop and the next few beads in the row to exit near the next loop. Repeat to attach all the loops on this half of the clasp, retrace the thread path, and end the tail.

6. Repeat steps 1–5 to make a second beaded tab and attach the other half of the clasp. Make sure the clasp half is positioned so it lines up correctly with the other clasp half.

7. Open an end link on one of the chains as you would a jump ring (Stringing Basics, p. 89), and attach it to a soldered jump ring on one of the beaded tabs **(photo 3)**. Close the link. Open the link on the other end of the same chain, and attach it to the corresponding soldered jump ring on the other beaded tab. Close the link.

8. Repeat step 7 to attach the remaining chains.

materials

bracelet 7½ in. (19.1 cm)
- **7** 6-in. (15 cm) lengths of chain with unsoldered links in assorted link sizes and finishes
- 5–6 g 10º cylinder beads
- **14** 4–6 mm soldered jump rings
- 7-strand slide clasp
- Fireline 6 lb. test

tools & supplies
- Stitching Toolbox, p. 89
- Stringing Toolbox, p. 89

techniques
- herringbone stitch

DVD review ▶
- Stringing: Opening and Closing Jump Rings
- Stitching: Ladder Stitch, Flat Herringbone Stitch

If you want to use chain with soldered links, sew through the end links of the chains instead of separate soldered jump rings.

Chains with different size links won't end up the same length. Use smaller jump rings at each end to even out the lengths.

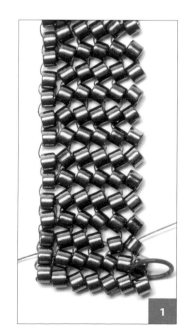

Modern warrior wear

Pat Benatar once warned us that "Love is a battlefield." **Theresa D. Abelew** says dress accordingly. Infuse the protective spirit of ancient armor with the element of surprise by zigzagging the classic European 4-in-1 chain mail weave. You'll catch any suitor, crafty compatriot, or last-minute guest off guard with your sharp style.

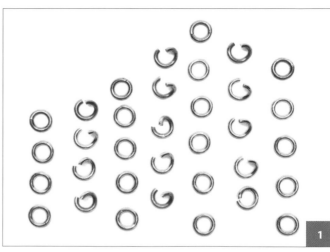

materials

bracelet 7¾ in. (19.7 cm)

- **306** ⁹⁄₆₄-in. (4 mm) inside-diameter (ID) aluminum jump rings, 18-gauge (1.0 mm)
- **172** ⁹⁄₆₄-in. (4 mm) ID bronze jump rings, 18-gauge (1.0 mm)
- 4-strand slide clasp

Jump rings (E18) and clasp from Blue Buddha Boutique, bluebuddhaboutique.com.

toolbox

- Wirework Basics, p. 91

techniques

- chain mail

DVD review ▶

- Stringing: Opening and Closing Jump Rings

A little prep work will speed up your weaving and help eliminate mistakes. Following the chart on p. 49, open and close the jump rings (Stringing Basics, p. 89) for the first 16 columns of the top half of the bracelet, and lay them out in their appropriate columns **(photo 1)**.

Top half

1. To begin the 4-in-1 pattern, pick up the bottom open aluminum ring in column 2. Slide two closed aluminum rings from column 1 and two from column 3 onto the open ring **(photo 2)**. Close the ring; you've just completed your first component. (Except for the edges of the bracelet, four rings will be woven through the center of every ring — this is how 4-in-1 earned its name.)

2. Position the component in a 2+1+2 configuration so that the outside columns are slanted opposite the center column **(photo 3)**.

Editor's note

When you open jump rings (Stringing Basics, p. 89), rotate the pliers in your dominant hand toward you. I'm right-handed, so I twist my right pliers to open jump rings, as shown by the blue jump ring above. This raises the right side of the ring, making it easier for me to pick it up and thread it into a pattern.

3. Slide the second open aluminum ring from column 2 through the top rings of columns 1 and 3 in the weave **(photo 4)**. Add one closed aluminum ring from column 1 and column 3. Close the ring. Split the two rings you just added, one to each side of the center ring **(photo 5)**.

4. Slide the third open ring from column 2 through the top rings of columns 1 and 3, and add column 1's closed bronze ring and the next aluminum ring from column 3. Close the ring. Split the two added rings, one to each side of the center ring **(photo 6)**.

5. Thread the open bronze ring from column 2 through the top two rings (bronze and aluminum), and add the closed bronze ring from column 3. Close the ring **(photo 7)**.

6. Slide the bottom open aluminum ring from column 4 through column 3's lower two aluminum rings. Add two closed aluminum rings from column 5. Close the ring **(photo 8)**. Repeat with the remaining rings from columns 4 and 5. Continue in this manner to connect the remaining columns in the first 16-column pattern.

To double-check your work, note that the bronze rings will mostly be a 3-in-1 pattern. However, due to the uneven column heights, column 5 will be a 2-in-1 pattern while column 13 is a 4-in-1.

7. Repeat the 16-column pattern three times. Start a fourth repeat, but end the weave after column 9 (the dotted line on the chart) **(photo 9)**.

Bottom half

Follow the chart to lay out the jump rings for the bottom half. Work as in steps 1–7 of "Top half" to create the bottom half of the weave.

Joining the halves

1. Align the two halves along the flat aluminum edge **(photo 10)**. To maintain the zigzag pattern, the column that's five aluminum rings high should line up directly across from the middle column that's one aluminum ring high (shaded boxes in the chart). Add or remove columns to adjust the length as needed. Keep in mind that the clasp will add about ½ in. (1.3 cm) to the bracelet.

Using two bronze rings, attach every other pair of aluminum rings, zipping the pieces together **(photo 11)**.

2. On each end of the bracelet, use aluminum rings to attach half of the clasp **(photo 12)**.

Design option

Slimming down. Instead of creating a straight edge and altering the number of jump rings in each column, as in the two halves of the large zigzag bracelet, make a narrow zigzag bracelet by attaching the same number of rings per column, staggering the starting point for each column.

9

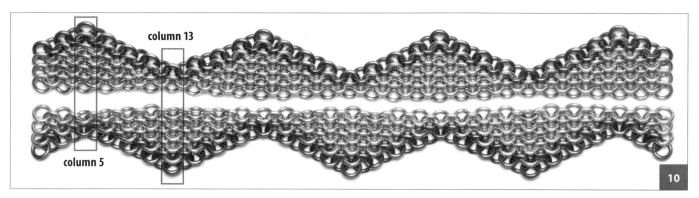

column 13

column 5

10

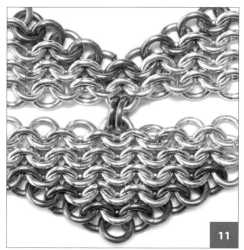

11

12

For a playful look, add color with anodized aluminum, niobium, or enameled copper jump rings.

Fun fact *Discovered in the graves of ancient Celtic warriors, some of the oldest examples of chain mail armor are more than 2,700 years old.*

COLUMN	1	2	3	4	5	6	7	8	9	10	11	12	13	14	15	16	
TOP HALF																	
jump rings	closed	open	closed	open	closed	open	closed	open	closed	open	closed	open	closed	open	closed	open	repeat
bronze	1	1	1	1	1	1	1	1	1	1	1	1	1	1	1	1	
aluminum	3	3	4	4	5	4	4	3	3	2	2	1	1	1	2	2	
BOTTOM HALF																	
jump rings	closed	open	closed	open	closed	open	closed	open	closed	open	closed	open	closed	open	closed	open	repeat
bronze	1	1	1	1	1	1	1	1	1	1	1	1	1	1	1	1	
aluminum	3	2	2	1	1	1	2	2	3	3	4	4	5	4	4	3	

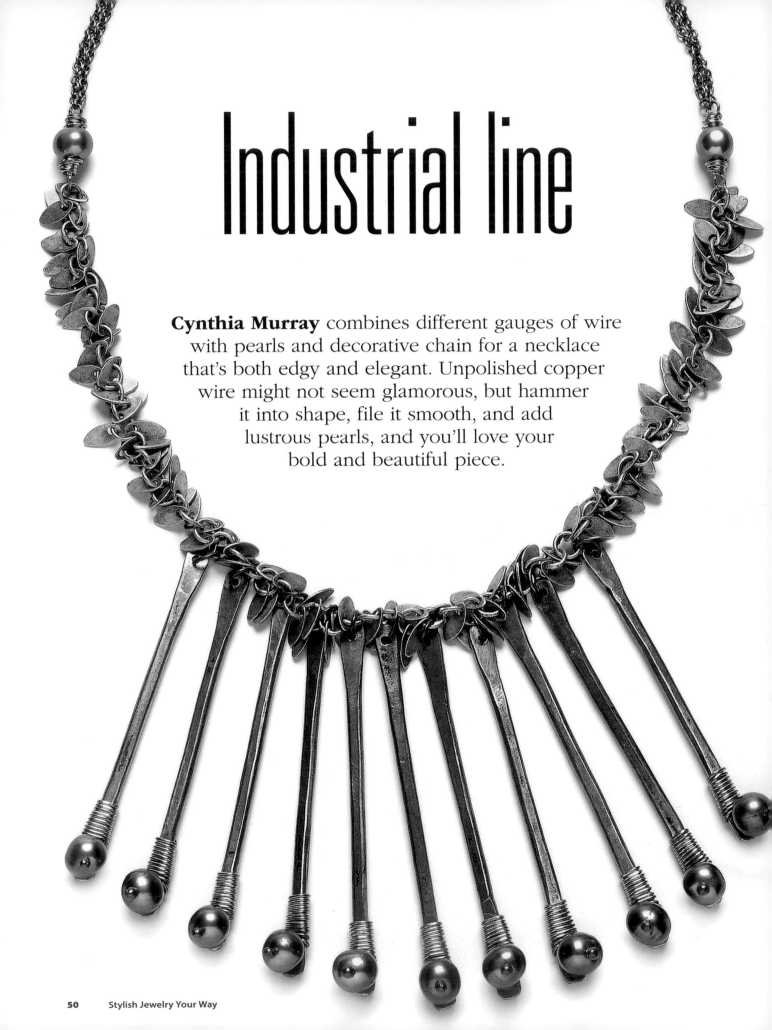

Industrial line

Cynthia Murray combines different gauges of wire with pearls and decorative chain for a necklace that's both edgy and elegant. Unpolished copper wire might not seem glamorous, but hammer it into shape, file it smooth, and add lustrous pearls, and you'll love your bold and beautiful piece.

Pearl sticks

1. Using heavy-duty wire cutters, cut 11 2½-in. (6.4 cm) pieces of 12-gauge wire. Straighten the wires.

2. Place a wire on a bench block or anvil, and hammer the ends into paddle shapes. Lightly hammer the entire length of the wire to flatten and work-harden the piece, making sure it stays straight as you work **(photo 1)**. Repeat with the other wires to create 11 wire sticks.

3. Use a file to refine the edges of each stick, rounding the paddle shapes and removing any burs or sharp edges.

4. Use a permanent marker to mark where you will punch a hole at each end of the sticks.

5. Using a hole punch or screw-down punch, make a hole at each mark **(photo 2)**.

6. If you are making your own head pins, cut 11 6-in. (15 cm) pieces of 22-gauge wire, then ball up the ends using a torch (Metalwork Basics, p. 92), or use roundnose pliers to turn a small loop at the end of each.

7. On a head pin, string a pearl and one hole of a stick. Wrap the wire around the stick about 10 times **(photo 3)**, keeping the wraps tight together. Trim the wire at the back of the stick, and press the end down with chainnose pliers. Repeat with the remaining pearls and sticks.

Assembly

1. Cut a 9-in. (23 cm) piece of decorative chain. Open 11 6 mm jump rings (Stringing Basics, p. 89).

2. Starting at the center of the chain, use a 6 mm jump ring to

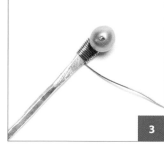

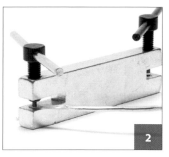

attach a pearl stick and a link of chain, and close the jump ring **(photo 4)**. On each side, skip a chain link, and repeat. Repeat with the remaining sticks and jump rings, attaching a total of five on each side of the center.

3. Cut four 3¼-in. (8.3 cm) pieces of cable chain and four 6-in. (15 cm) pieces of 22-gauge wire.

4. Using one of the wires, make the first half of a wrapped loop (Wirework Basics, p. 91) 2½ in. (6.4 cm) from one end of the wire. Attach an end link of the decorative chain, and complete the wraps, making a second layer of wraps over the first. String a pearl on the wire, and make the first half of a wrapped loop. Attach an end link of two pieces of cable chain, and complete the wraps as you did before. Repeat on the other end of the decorative chain.

5. Using one of the remaining wires, make the first half of a wrapped loop, and attach the remaining end links of the two cable chains at one end of the necklace. Complete the wraps, and string a pearl. Make the first half of a wrapped loop, attach half of the clasp, and complete the wraps. Repeat this step on the other end of the necklace.

> *Make sure your wire is half-hard or dead-soft. Regular hardware store copper wire might be too hard to work with.*

Design *option*

Stick 'em up. Two pearl sticks, either plain or adorned with a bit of decorative chain, can make long, eye-catching earrings. The wire shown here is 16-gauge black annealed steel from the hardware store; the maple-leaf chain is from Chelsea's Beads, chelseasbeads.com.

materials

necklace 19 in. (48 cm)
- 28 in. (71 cm) 12-gauge copper, silver, or aluminum wire, half-hard
- **15** 6–8 mm pearls
- 9½ in. (24.1 cm) decorative chain
- 14 in. (36 cm) cable chain
- **11** 3–4-in. (7.6–10 cm) decorative head pins, or 2 yd. (1.8 m) 22-gauge wire
- 24 in. (61 cm) 22-gauge wire
- **11** 6 mm jump rings
- clasp

Leaf chain from AD Adornments, adadornments.com. Check your local bead store for other supplies.

tools & supplies

- Metalwork Toolbox, p. 92
- Wirework Toolbox, p. 91
- heavy-duty wire cutters
- permanent marker
- hole punch or screw-down punch
- butane torch (optional)

techniques

- metalwork
- wirework

DVD review ▶

- Stringing: Opening and Closing Jump Rings
- Wirework: Wrapped Loop
- Metalwork: Balling the End of a Wire

Lovely latch-backs

The first time she saw a pair of earrings with latch-back findings, **Leanne Elliott Soden** couldn't wait to make her own. After a bit of experimenting, she was hooked. For these earrings, either purchase metal disks or use a disk cutter to cut your own from metal sheet. To keep things easy, make the holes in the center of the disks with hole-punch pliers. Basic wireworking skills take care of the rest.

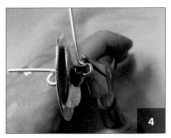

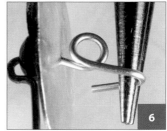

Pinwheel disks

You'll need two large and two small metal disks. I made the large disks and bought the small disks; you can make or buy disks as desired.

1. To make the two large disks, use a disk cutter to cut two ¾-in. (1.9 cm) disks from 24-gauge (0.51 mm) sterling silver sheet. Using hole-punch pliers, make a 1 mm hole through the center of each disk **(photo 1)**. Use a flat file to remove any burrs around each hole.

2. Place the disks on a bench block. Use the round face of a ball-peen hammer to repeatedly strike the disk with even, overlapping blows **(photo 2)**. File the edges of the disks smooth with a hand file.

3. If you didn't purchase your small disks, make two small disks.

Assembly

1. Cut a 4-in. (10 cm) piece of 20-gauge sterling silver wire. Using roundnose pliers, grasp the wire ⅜ in. (1 cm) from one end. Wrap the wire around one jaw of the pliers to form a loop **(photo 3)**.

2. Using 400-grit sandpaper, smooth and round the wire end closest to the loop. Slide a large disk onto the long end of the wire. The back of the disk should face the loop. Add a small metal disk and a 3–4 mm bead.

3. Using chainnose pliers, grasp the working wire in front of the bead, and make a series of three tight 90-degree bends **(photo 4)**. The working wire should be perpendicular to the looped wire at the back of the earring.

4. Measure the working wire ⅜ in. (1 cm) from the edge of the large disk, and bend the wire over a dowel or pen at this point **(photo 5)**, making sure that the working wire lines up with the loop at the back of the earring.

5. Using roundnose pliers, grasp the short, looped wire ⁵⁄₃₂ in. (4 mm) from its end, and make a U bend toward the back of the earring **(photo 6)**. This is the catch for your ear wire **(figure)**.

6. Press the ear wire into the catch, and trim the excess wire ⅜–⁹⁄₁₆ in. (1–1.4 cm) below the catch. Smooth the end of the ear wire with 400-grit sandpaper.

7. Repeat steps 1–6 to make the second earring.

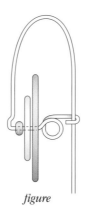

figure

Want to cut your own disks? You can learn how to use a disk cutter on the DVD included with this book.

materials

pair of earrings
- 1 x 2 in. (2.5 x 5 cm) 24-gauge (0.51 mm) sterling silver sheet, dead-soft; or 2 ¾-in. (1.9 cm) 24-gauge sterling silver disks
- 2 ½-in. (1.3 cm) 24-gauge (0.5 mm) sterling silver disks, center drilled
- 8 in. (20 cm) 20-gauge (0.81 mm) round sterling silver wire, half-hard
- 2 3–4 mm beads

Precut disks available from Santa Fe Jewelers Supply, (800) 659-3835, sfjssantafe.com.

tools & supplies
- Wirework Toolbox, p. 91
- Metalwork Toolbox, p. 92
- disk cutters: large, small (optional)
- hole-punch pliers (optional)
- dowel or pen

techniques
- metalwork
- wirework

Design *option*

One-of-a-kind pinwheels. Instead of using metal disks for the earrings' pinwheel components, try combining other drilled, flat objects like stone, Lucite, glass, seashells, vintage buttons, wood, or crystal. You could even mix and match components so the pinwheels in each earring look similar but don't match exactly.

Urban armor

Anna Elizabeth Draeger stitched this stylish and substantial cuff with peanut beads and right-angle weave. Embed crystals and pearls in this thick band to add a bit of subtle glamour.

materials

bracelet 7 in. (18 cm)
- 17.5 g 2 x 4 mm peanut beads (P4018, matte pebble)
- **112** 3 mm round pearls in each of **2** colors: A (Swarovski, jet black), B (Swarovski, dark gray)
- **56** 3 mm round crystals, color C (Swarovski, greige)
- 5-strand slide clasp
- **10** 6 mm jump rings
- Fireline 6 lb. test

tools & supplies
- Stitching Toolbox, p. 89
- Stringing Toolbox, p. 89

techniques
- right-angle weave

DVD review
- Stringing: Opening and Closing Jump Rings
- Stitching: Ending and Adding Thread, Overhand Knot, Flat Right Angle Weave

Fun fact

Peanut beads are also called butterfly, dog-bone, farfalle, bowtie, barbell, and berry beads.

Design option

Think thin. Make narrow cuffs three stitches wide, using peanut beads for the edge stitches and an accent bead and a peanut bead for the center stitch. Join the end stitches to make a bangle, or attach a single-loop clasp as for the wide cuff.

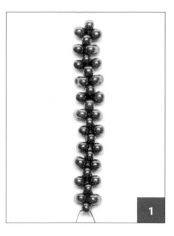

1. On a comfortable length of Fireline, pick up four 2 x 4 mm peanut beads, leaving a 6-in. (15 cm) tail. Tie the beads into a ring with a square knot (Stitching Basics, p. 89).

2. Work a strip of 11 stitches in right-angle weave (Stitching Basics) using peanut beads. Zigzag back through the strip **(photo 1)**.

3. Sew through the last stitch to exit a side peanut bead. Working in right-angle weave, add a row (Stitching Basics) using three peanut beads for the first stitch, and two beads per stitch to complete the row as follows:
Stitch 2: a color A 3 mm pearl and a peanut **(photo 2)**.
Stitch 3: two peanuts

Stitch 4: a color B 3 mm pearl and a peanut
Stitch 5: two peanuts
Stitch 6: a color C round crystal and a peanut
Stitch 7: two peanuts
Stitch 8: a B and a peanut
Stitch 9: two peanuts
Stitch 10: an A and a peanut
Stitch 11: two peanuts
Zigzag back through the row **(photo 3)**.

4. Add a row as in step 3, but in the stitches with 3 mm accent beads, pick up a peanut bead first and then the accent bead.

5. Repeat steps 3 and 4 to the desired length, ending and adding thread (Stitching Basics) as needed.

6. Work the last row using all peanut beads. End the working thread and tail.

7. Open a 6 mm jump ring (Stringing Basics, p. 89), and attach an end stitch and a loop of half of the clasp **(photo 4)**. Close the jump ring. Repeat to attach the remaining loops of this half of the clasp. Attach the other half of the clasp on the other end of the bracelet.

If you lose your place as you repeat steps 3 and 4, remember this: If you are exiting a peanut bead, pick up an accent bead first, and if you are exiting an accent bead, pick up a peanut bead first.

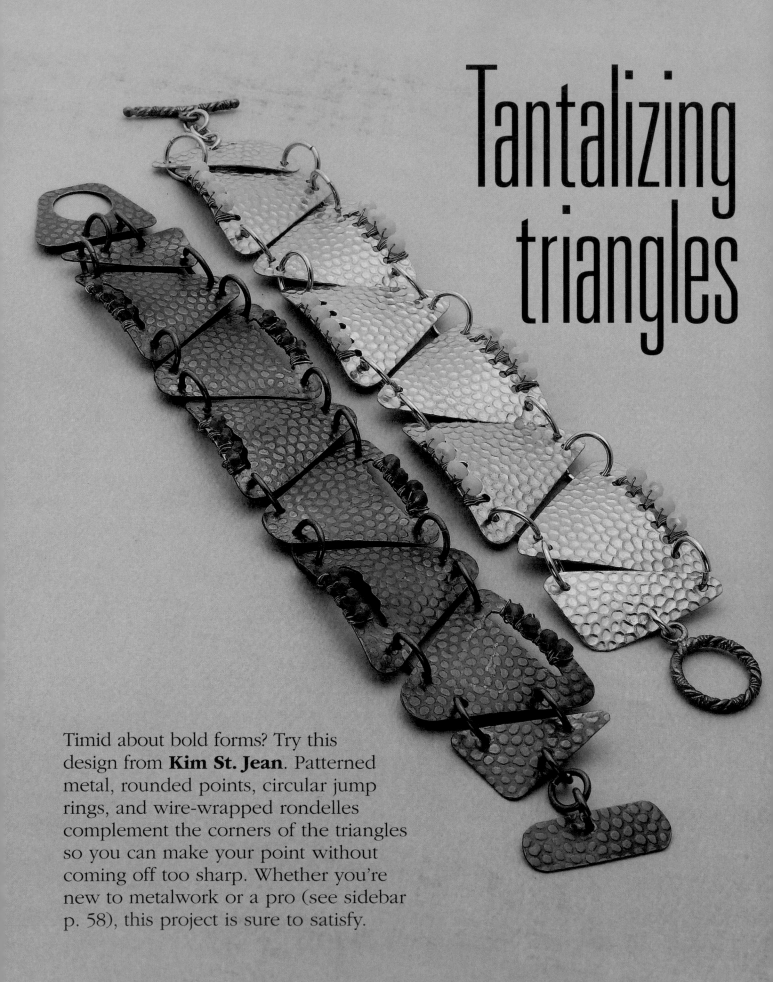

Tantalizing triangles

Timid about bold forms? Try this design from **Kim St. Jean**. Patterned metal, rounded points, circular jump rings, and wire-wrapped rondelles complement the corners of the triangles so you can make your point without coming off too sharp. Whether you're new to metalwork or a pro (see sidebar p. 58), this project is sure to satisfy.

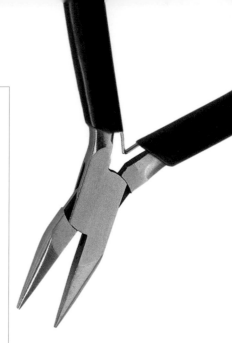

1. Make a copy of the **template** below. Cut out each triangle. Using rubber cement or double-sided tape, adhere each triangle to the 24-gauge patterned copper strip, leaving a little space between them.

2. Using metal shears, cut out each triangle. To save yourself some cutting, align an edge of the triangle with an edge of the copper strip **(photo 1)**. You can also place the triangles edge to edge so you only have to make one cut between them.

3. Punch holes as indicated on the templates **(photo 2)**, then peel off the templates.

4. Sand the edges of the triangles. Use a needle file to smooth the holes.

5. If desired, add a patina to the triangles with liver of sulfur (Metalwork Basics, p. 92).

6. Using your hands or bracelet-bending pliers, curve each triangle gently.

7. Locate the side of a large triangle with seven holes. (The two outer holes are for jump rings, and the five inner holes are for wire wrapping.) Cut a 12-in. (30 cm) piece of 28-gauge wire, and thread it through the first inner hole, leaving a 1-in. (2.5 cm) tail. Wrap the wire through the hole three times **(photo 3)**.

8. String a 3 mm rondelle, and wrap the wire through the next hole twice **(photo 4)**. Repeat this step to add three more beads, wrapping the wire three times through the last inner hole. Thread the wire under the wraps on the back surface of the triangle once or twice **(photo 5)**, and trim the excess wire. Repeat with the tail.

materials

bracelet 8 in. (20 cm)

- 12 x 2½-in. (30 x 6.4 cm) 24-gauge patterned copper strip
- 24 3 mm rondelles
- 6 ft. (1.8 m) 28-gauge copper wire
- 14 10 mm jump rings
- 4 7 mm jump rings
- toggle clasp

Patterned copper strip from Metalliferous, store.metalliferous.com.

tools & supplies

- Metalwork Toolbox, p. 92
- Stringing Toolbox, p. 89
- rubber cement or double-sided tape
- 1.8 mm hole-punch pliers
- bracelet-bending pliers (optional)

techniques

- metalwork
- wirework

DVD review ▶

- Stringing: Opening and Closing Jump Rings
- Metalwork: Adding Patina with Liver of Sulfur

If you have sharp edges around the punched holes on the back of the triangles, use chainnose or flat-nose pliers to gently press them down.

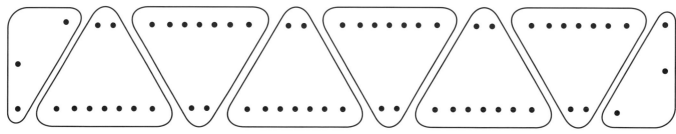

template

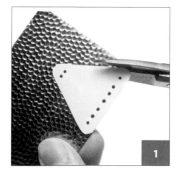

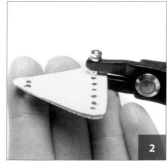

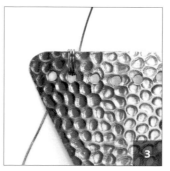

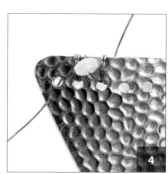

9. Repeat steps 7 and 8 with the remaining triangles.

10. Lay out the large triangles, alternating the embellished edges. On each end, lay out a small triangle.

11. Open a 10 mm jump ring (Stringing Basics, p. 89), and attach two adjacent holes on a pair of neighboring triangles. Close the jump ring. Repeat to attach the other adjacent holes on the triangles **(photo 6)**. Continue attaching all the triangles in the bracelet.

12. Open a 7 mm jump ring, and attach the toggle ring to the remaining hole on a small triangle. Close the jump ring. Use a chain of three 5 mm jump rings to attach the toggle bar to the other small triangle **(photo 7)**.

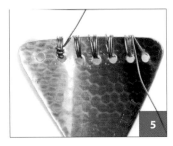
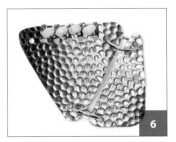

5

6

7

Budget *option*

Waste not. Put your leftover patterned metal to work: Cut out shapes for earrings, pendants, or charms. These 2½ x ½-in. (6.4 x 1.3 cm) paddle earrings are long on style but not on work.

Got a bench? Get to work!

If you have a well-stocked metalwork bench at your disposal, here are four great ways to put it to use in this project:

1. Use a rolling mill and texture sheet to add a pattern to plain 24-gauge metal sheet. You can also texture the metal with a texture hammer.

2. Rather than wrapping the wire through a series of five holes, cut an oval opening along one edge of each large triangle using a jeweler's saw.

3. Make your own jump rings: Use 16-gauge wire and a Wrap 'n' Tap tool to make a coil, then use a jeweler's saw to cut the rings apart.

4. Cut out shapes to make your own toggle clasp, (right) using a disk cutter to create a large opening for the toggle ring.

Bohemian Beauty

Soak up the Renaissance-inspired colors and textures of this jewelry, and you're sure to feel your free-spirited side surface. These projects offer many chances to experiment with techniques including making beaded beads, creating metal clay charms, setting favorite trinkets in resin, and pushing creative boundaries with flowing bead embroidery.

Let it slide

Julia Gerlach's interchangeable beaded beads are a snap to make and easily slide onto ribbons. Wear your necklace short or long, with the ends in front or back, or add additional large-hole beads for a style that's all your own.

Design *option*

Beaded bead

1. On 18 in. (46 cm) of Fireline, pick up a repeating pattern of an 11º seed bead and a color A 4 mm fire-polished bead six times, leaving a 6-in. (15 cm) tail. Tie the beads into a ring with a square knot (Stitching Basics, p. 89). Sew through the 4 mms only **(figure a)**, and pull them together to make the 11ºs pop out slightly.

2. Pick up five 15º seed beads, and sew through the 4 mm

your thread just exited and the next 4 mm **(figure b)**.

3. Pick up four 15ºs, and sew through the adjacent 15º in the previous stitch, the 4 mm your thread just exited, and the next 4 mm **(figure c)**.

4. Repeat step 3 three times **(figure d)**, then sew through the adjacent 15º in the first stitch of 15ºs.

5. Pick up three 15ºs, and sew through the adjacent 15º in the previous stitch, the 4 mm your thread just exited, and the next 4 mm **(figure e)**.

6. Repeat steps 2–5 on the other side of the ring of 4 mms, and end the working thread and tail (Stitching Basics).

Necklace

1. Make a total of three beaded beads with 4 mms as explained in "Beaded bead."

2. Make three more beaded beads as follows:
• Substitute 6 mms for the 4 mms (make one each with color B, C, and D 6 mms).
• Pick up seven 15ºs in step 2, six 15ºs per stitch in steps 3 and 4, and five 15ºs in step 5.

3. Gather the silk ribbons together, and string five beaded beads in the following order: color A, color B, color C, color D, color A.

4. On one end of the ribbons, string the remaining color A beaded bead. Pass the other end of the ribbons through it in the opposite direction.

Change it up.
To wear your necklace lariat-style, hold the ends of all the ribbons in a tight bundle, and string the beaded beads in the desired order over the entire bundle.

○ 4 mm fire-polished bead

● 11º seed bead

● 15º seed bead

materials

necklace 16–32 in. (41–81 cm)

- **3** 32–36-in. (.8–.9 m) ½-in. (1.3 cm) wide silk ribbons (Mediterranean blue, burnt orange, and autumn leaves blend)
- Czech fire-polished beads
  - **18** 4 mm, color A (turquoise Picasso)
  - **6** 6 mm in each of **3** colors: B (carnelian opal), C (light ochre matte metallic), D (Indian yellow opal)
- 1 g 11º seed beads (457L, metallic light bronze)
- 2 g 15º seed beads (457L, metallic light bronze)
- Fireline 6 lb. test

tools & supplies

- Stitching Toolbox, p. 89

techniques

- netting

DVD review ▶

- Stitching: Ending and Adding Thread, Square Knot

To achieve a sturdy beaded bead, pull each stitch tight before working the next one.

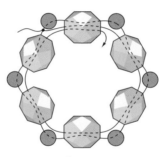

figure a

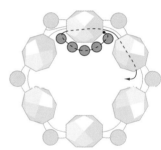

figure b

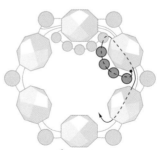

figure c

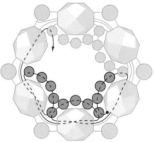

figure d

figure e

First time's a charm

Irina Miech has been teaching metal clay classes for 15 years and still enjoys witnessing the thrill beginners get when they see their finished pieces. This project is a great way to dip your toe in if you are curious about creating with metal clay. Don't worry if you don't have a kiln; many bead stores (or art departments at colleges) will fire your pieces for a nominal fee.

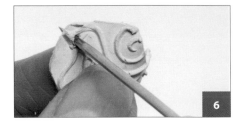

8. Burnish the fired piece with a polishing brush and soapy water to create a shiny surface. Finish with a polishing cloth if desired.

Metal clay pendants or charms

1. Form about 6–8 g of clay into a ball. Apply a thin layer of balm to the clay.

2. Apply a thin layer of balm to your roller and work surface. Stack four playing cards on each side of the clay and roll out the clay to the thickness of the card stacks.

3. With the roller, press the clay onto a texture sheet. remove the clay and place a leaf vein side down on the untextured side. Stack three cards and imprint the leaf pattern with the roller.

4. Use a tissue blade or craft knife to cut out a leaf shape.

5. Let the charm dry completely. To curve the charm, drape it over a pen or pencil as it dries.

6. After the piece is dry, twist the tip of the knife to make a hole. Smooth the edges with a metal file.

7. Use a fine-grade sanding pad to smooth the edges. Fire your piece according to the manufacturer's directions.

- *Lump clay can dry out quickly. Keep unused portions in plastic wrap, and mist with water to moisten the clay you're working with as needed.*
- *Your finished piece will be slightly smaller than when you put it in the kiln; PMC3 shrinks about 12% in volume when fired.*

8 Use a jump ring to attach a hook clasp to the other end.

7 Attach the head pin unit to the end link of the chain. Complete the wraps.

1

head pin unit
On a head pin, string a pearl. Make the first half of a wrapped loop (Wirework Basics, p. 91).

necklace
Make the head pin unit and bead units (right). Cut a 6-in. (15 cm), a 3-in. (7.6 cm), a 2-in. (5 cm), and two ½-in. (1.3 cm) pieces of chain.

bead unit
Cut a 3-in. (7.6 cm) piece of 24-gauge wire. Make the first half of a wrapped loop (Wirework Basics, p. 91). String a 9–12 mm bead and make the first half of a wrapped loop. Make three or four 9–12 mm bead units and six to eight rondelle units.

6 On the last loop, attach the 6-in. (15 cm) chain. Complete the wraps.

2 On one end of the 3-in. (7.6 cm) chain, attach: bead unit, ½-in. (1.3 cm) chain, bead unit, ½-in. (1.3 cm) chain, bead unit. Complete the wraps as you go, leaving the last loop open.

5 Attach the rondelle units, completing the wraps as you go. Leave the last loop open.

3 On the last loop, attach the 2-in. (5 cm) chain and complete the wraps.

4 Open a jump ring (Stringing Basics, p. 89). Attach the charm and the center link of the 2-in. (5 cm) chain. Close the jump ring.

The patina on the metal clay charms was created by dipping them in a liver of sulfur (LOS) solution.

How-to: Add about 1 tsp. of LOS crystals or gel and 1 tsp. of ammonia to very hot, but not boiling, water. Use tweezers to quickly dip a charm in the solution and then in clean, cold water. Dry the charm. Check the color and repeat until you achieve the desired effect. You can polish off areas of the patina with a polishing pad, brush, or cloth.

If you're making a curved charm, fire it in a bowl of vermiculite so the piece doesn't flatten on the floor of the kiln.

materials

necklace 17 in. (43 cm)

- silver metal clay (one package)
- **3–4** 9–12 mm beads
- 6–8 mm potato pearl
- **6–8** 6 mm rondelles
- 27–36 in. (69–90 cm) 24-gauge half-hard wire
- 12 in. (30 cm) chain, 4–5 mm links
- 1½-in. (3.8 cm) head pin
- **2** 7 mm jump rings
- hook clasp

tools & supplies

- Stringing Toolbox, p. 89
- Metal Clay Toolbox, p. 92
- texture sheet and leaf
- pen or pencil (optional)
- polishing cloth (optional)

techniques

- stringing
- metal clay

DVD review ▶

- Stringing: Opening and Closing Jump Rings
- Wirework: Wrapped Loop
- Metalwork: Adding Patina with Liver of Sulfur
- Clays and Resin: Rolling and Cutting Metal Clay, Texturing Metal Clay, Torch-Firing Metal Clay

A kiln — even a small one — is an investment. Kiln-firing is usually the best option so, if possible, bring your piece to a local bead store to fire for a small fee. Check with the store for restrictions on firing.

Torch-firing

Torch-firing is an option for this project. To do this, use a small butane torch — often available in kitchen stores — and a firing brick. Place the unfired metal clay piece in the middle of a firing brick. Dim the lights and hold the torch at a 45 degree angle 2 in. (5 cm) from the piece. You will see a small amount of smoke and flame, and then the piece will turn white. Keep the torch moving over the piece until you see the piece glow. When the piece turns a peach color, begin timing the firing. Firing time ranges from 1–5 minutes, depending on weight. The charm in this project uses about 8 grams of clay, so it should take about 90 seconds. When finished, use tweezers to move your piece to the cooler edge of the firing brick and allow it to cool.

Metal clay pieces must be under 25 grams in weight and no larger than a United States silver dollar to be torch fired. You cannot torch fire pieces if the main component is sheet or paper clay or if the piece is formed around cork clay. Torch-firing with cork clay can create open flames and is hazardous.

Double vision

Always one to greet a challenge to gain an opportunity, **Susan Lenart Kazmer** shows how to create a two-sided pendant using resin in an open-back bezel. For the clown pendant, she flipped the bezel upside down and drilled two holes for a handmade wire bail. But for a first foray into filling open-back bezels with resin, you can simplify the process and skip the bail. For some tips, check out the list of do's and don'ts (p. 68) as well as Clay and Resin Basics, p. 92, and the DVD before you get started.

Pendant

1. Cut a piece of packing tape to fit over the back of an open-back bezel. Press the tape along the back of the bezel. Use a craft stick to burnish the tape to create a tight seal.

Cut two images to fit back-to-back in the bezel. Using a sponge applicator, coat each side of each image with paper sealer and allow to dry for about six hours.

2. Following the manufacturer's directions, mix a small batch of ICE Resin.

Place the bezel on a flat surface. Using the tip of the craft stick, drip resin to cover the bottom ¼ of the bezel.

3. Place an image face down in the bezel. Slowly drip in more resin. Place another image face up in the bezel so when you remove the packing tape,

you'll have a double-sided focal for your piece.

For a shallow bezel, drip resin to the top. Allow to fully cure for three days. Remove the tape from the back of the bezel.

For a deep bezel, drip resin until the bezel is ¾ full. Allow to cure. Mix a new batch of resin. Drip resin to the top of the bezel. Allow to cure. Remove the tape.

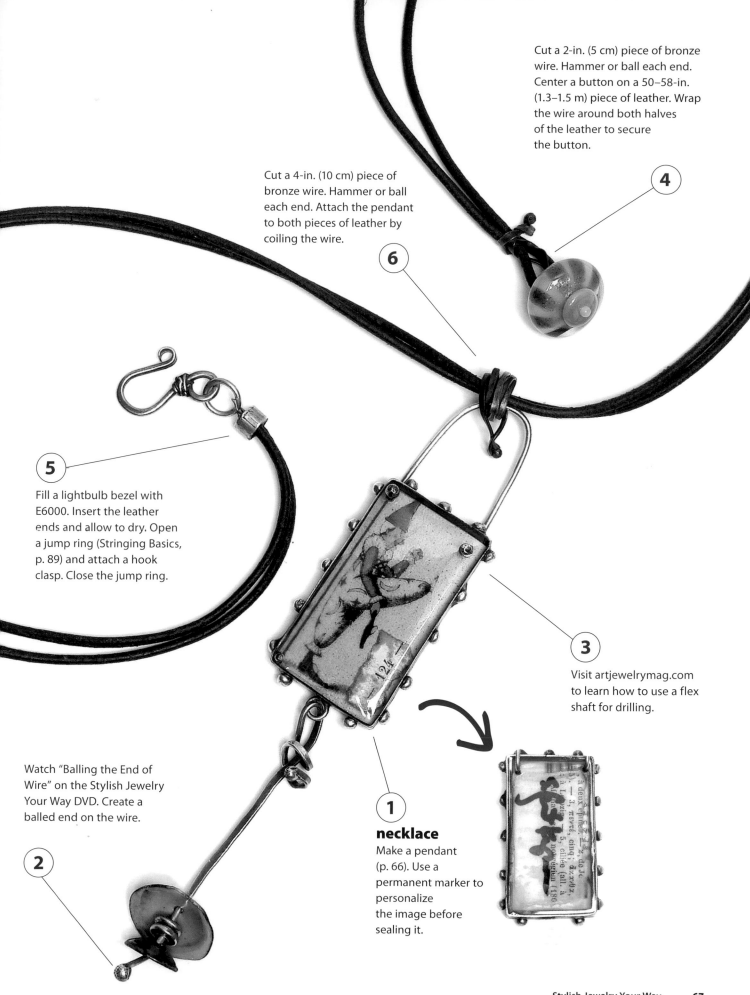

Cut a 2-in. (5 cm) piece of bronze wire. Hammer or ball each end. Center a button on a 50–58-in. (1.3–1.5 m) piece of leather. Wrap the wire around both halves of the leather to secure the button.

4

Cut a 4-in. (10 cm) piece of bronze wire. Hammer or ball each end. Attach the pendant to both pieces of leather by coiling the wire.

6

Fill a lightbulb bezel with E6000. Insert the leather ends and allow to dry. Open a jump ring (Stringing Basics, p. 89) and attach a hook clasp. Close the jump ring.

5

Visit artjewelrymag.com to learn how to use a flex shaft for drilling.

3

Watch "Balling the End of Wire" on the Stylish Jewelry Your Way DVD. Create a balled end on the wire.

2

1

necklace
Make a pendant (p. 66). Use a permanent marker to personalize the image before sealing it.

Do:

- Use a craft stick to burnish the back of the taped bezel (**photo 1**).

- After slowly and thoroughly mixing the resin for two minutes, allow it to sit for five minutes before dripping it into the bezel.

- Layer the images close to the surface of each side of a deep bezel (**photo 2**).

- Use images with a lot of contrast. Otherwise, especially in a deep pendant, the details get lost.

- Nearly fill the bezel and let the resin dry for six hours. Resin in a deep bezel will overflow if you try to dome it in one pour. Mix up a new batch of resin and drip in a layer to dome.

Don't:

- Pour resin into the bezel directly from a cup. Instead, drip small amounts of resin from the tip of a craft stick (**photo 3**).

- Wait to clean up spilled resin. You have 30–45 minutes before it starts to harden (**photo 4**).

For more tips and techniques, visit iceresin.com.

materials

pendant

- 15–45 mm bezel with loop
- diagonal wire cutters
- ICE Resin
- Art Mechanique paper sealer
- images to fit inside bezel
- packing tape
- plastic gloves
- waxed paper

necklace 28 in. (71 cm)

- pendant
- 18 mm glass button
- 50–58 in. (1.3–1.5 m) 2 mm leather cord
- 6 in. (15 cm) 18-gauge bronze wire
- 6 mm lightbulb bezel
- hook clasp
- 9 mm jump ring
- **2** pairs of pliers
- E6000 adhesive
- hammer
- bench block or anvil

Glass button by Michele Goldstein, michelegoldstein.com. Bezels and ICE Resin available from www.iceresin.com.

tools & supplies

- Stringing Toolbox, p. 89
- Clays and Resin Toolbox p. 92

techniques

- stringing
- resin

DVD review ▶

- Wirework: Wrapped Loop
- Metalwork: Balling the End of a Wire
- Clays and Resin: Using Resin

Design *option*

Try different bezel styles. These square frame bezels are perfect for lightweight earrings.

Ebb
and flow

Dive into bead embroidery by using a variety of techniques, and let your imagination guide you. **Tea Benduhn** mimics the shimmer of water with a silver fabric foundation for her design, letting it peek through the beadwork.

Design *option*

Brooch the subject. For a mini bead-embroidered piece, make a brooch. Work the bead embroidery as for a necklace. Sew a pin-back finding to the Ultrasuede before completing the assembly of the brooch.

Preparation

1. Determine the finished length and shape of your necklace, and sketch a rough outline onto cardstock. Within the rough outline, further define the islands that will later be connected to form the necklace. Cut out the islands, and trace them onto the fabric and the Ultrasuede using a permanent marker.

2. Tape or glue your cabochons and larger beads to the fabric as desired.

Bead-embroidery techniques

This is a free-form piece that incorporates a variety of bead-embroidery techniques. Fill in each island as desired, selecting from the techniques below. Sew to the edge of the outline, being sure to cover the marker lines with beads.

Make an overhand knot (Stitching Basics, p. 89) on one end of 1 yd. (.9 m) of thread, and sew up through the fabric next to where you want to begin stitching. For all steps below, end and add thread as needed (Stitching Basics). End all threads when finished.

Beaded backstitch

1. Pick up two or three cylinder or seed beads, lay them along the fabric as desired, and sew down through the fabric next to the last bead **(photo 1)**.

2. Sew up through the fabric between the first and second beads. Sew through the last one or two beads again.

3. Repeat steps 1 and 2 as desired.

Making a cabochon bezel

1. Sew up through the fabric next to the cabochon. Work a round of beaded backstitch around the cab, picking up two cylinders per stitch to end with an even number of cylinders in the round.

2. Pick up a cylinder, skip a cylinder, and sew through the next cylinder **(photo 2)**. Work in tubular peyote stitch (Stitching Basics) to complete the round, stepping up through the first cylinder added in the new round.

3. Repeat step 2 to add as many rounds as needed for the height of your cab.

4. Work one or two rounds of peyote stitch with 15º seed beads, snugging up the bead-work to the top of your cab.

5. Sew through the beadwork

to exit the first round, and sew down through the fabric.

Adding a large bead

Sew up through the fabric next to one hole of the large bead, and sew through the bead. Sew down through the fabric next to the end of the hole. Sew through the bead and fabric again **(photo 3)**.

Adding an accent bead

Pick up a small bead, and sew down through the fabric next to the bead **(photo 4)**.

Brace(let) yourself. To make a bracelet, sew each half of a clasp to each end of the bracelet, hiding the holes of the clasp between the layers of fabric and Ultrasuede.

Design **option**

materials

necklace 20 in. (51 cm)
- **3** 25–50 mm cabochons
- **100–200** 3–10 mm assorted accent beads, disks, lentils, freshwater pearls, fringe drops, and gemstones
- 7–12 g 11º cylinder beads in a variety of colors
- 7–12 g 11º seed beads in a variety of colors
- 7–12 g 15º seed beads in a variety of colors
- clasp
- 7 x 7 in. (18 x 18 cm) fabric
- 7 x 7 in. (18 x 18 cm) Ultrasuede
- 7 x 7 in. (18 x 18 cm) cardstock
- nylon beading thread, size D, in a color to match fabric, or Fireline 6 lb. test

tools & supplies
- Stitching Toolbox, p. 89
- double-sided tape or E6000 adhesive
- permanent marker

techniques
- bead embroidery

DVD review ▶
- Stitching Basics: Overhand Knot, Tubular Peyote Stitch

Button stitch

Pick up a bead and a 15º seed bead. Skip the 15º, and sew back through the bead and the fabric where your needle exited **(photo 5).**

Adding disk beads, fringe drops, or lentils

Sew as in "Beaded backstitch" or "Adding an accent bead," picking up one to three beads at a time. Pull the thread taut to make sure the beads are positioned the way you want them.

Assembly

1. Trim the fabric close to the edge of your beadwork, taking care not to cut the thread.

2. Cut the Ultrasuede to match the bead-embroidered fabric.

3. Tape or glue the Ultrasuede to the back of the cardstock and the embroidered fabric to the front of the cardstock. If using glue, let it dry.

Edging

1. Sew between the two layers of fabric, and exit the top surface. Pick up three 11º or 15º seed beads, and sew back down through the fabric and Ultrasuede two bead widths from where your thread exited. Sew back through the third 11º or 15º. Repeat around the edge, but pick up only two 11ºs or 15ºs per stitch **(photo 6).** When you reach the first stitch, pick up an 11º or 15º, and sew down

through the first 11º or 15º, the fabric, and the Ultrasuede. Sew back up through the 11º or 15º and the next 11º or 15º.

2. To work a second row, pick up an 11º or 15º, and sew through the middle 11º or 15º in the next edging stitch. Repeat around, and end the thread.

Joining islands

Sew through an edge bead. Pick up an 11º or 15º seed bead, an accent bead, and an 11º or 15º. Sew through the corresponding edge bead of the next island. Sew through the beadwork to exit the edge

bead your thread just entered, sew back through the 11º or 15º, accent bead, 11º or 15º, and the edge bead of the first island your thread exited. Retrace the thread path.

Necklace strands

Sew through an edge bead where you want to attach your neck straps. Pick up assorted beads for the desired length and half of a clasp. Sew back through the beads just picked up and the edge bead your thread just exited. Retrace the thread path. Repeat for as many strands as desired, and end the thread. Repeat on the remaining side.

Butterfly effect

Jane Danley Cruz designed this necklace with two or more colors of beads to complement a focal piece and add texture for contemporary style. Made with 6º and 8º seed beads, this necklace comes together quickly.

Russian spiral

1. On a comfortable length of Fireline, pick up two 8º seed beads, a color A 6º seed bead, two 8ºs, and an A, leaving an 8-in. (20 cm) tail. Sew through the first 8º again to form a ring **(figure a)**.

2. Pick up an A and two 8ºs, skip the next 8º and A in the ring, and sew through the following 8º **(figure b)**.

3. Pick up an A and two 8ºs, skip the next 8º and A in the previous round, and sew through the following 8º. Step up through the next A and 8º **(figure c)** to begin the next round.

4. Repeat step 3 for 4 in. (10 cm), then continue as in steps 2 and 3, using color B 6º seed beads in place of the As for 10 in. (25 cm). End and add thread (Stitching Basics, p. 89) as needed.

5. To finish the rope, continue as in steps 2 and 3 using As instead of Bs for 4 in. (10 cm).

6. Pick up one side of a wire guard, a 6 mm split ring, and the other side of the wire guard, and sew through all the beads in the last round of the rope. Retrace the thread path, and end the thread.

7. With the tail, repeat step 6 on the other end of the rope.

Focal and clasp

1. Open an 8 mm jump ring (Stringing Basics, p. 89), and attach one hole of the focal and one end of an 8 x 18 mm connector. Close the jump ring. Use a 6 mm split ring to attach the other end of the connector to one end of the rope.

2. Open a 4 mm jump ring, and attach a B to the 6 mm split ring. Close the jump ring.

3. Open an 8 mm jump ring, and attach the remaining hole of the focal and a 6 mm split ring. Close the jump ring.

4. Attach a 6 mm split ring to the remaining end of the rope. Attach one half of the clasp to each of the split rings on this end of the rope/focal.

5. Embellish the 6 mm split rings on this end of the rope as in step 2.

materials

necklace 23½ in. (59.7 cm)
- 56 x 38 mm butterfly ceramic focal by Mary Poineal
- 8–10 g 6º seed beads in each of **2** colors: A (Matsuno 5686, iris green), B (Matsuno 5953, transparent jade green)
- 8–10 g 8º seed beads (Matsuno 4487, iris bronze)
- 8 x 18 mm deco window brass connector
- **2** wire guards
- **2** 8 mm jump rings (antique copper)
- **3** 6 mm split rings (antique copper)
- **3** 4 mm jump rings (antique copper)
- 12 mm lobster claw clasp with tab (antique copper)
- Fireline 6 lb. test

Butterfly focal available from foremostfocal.com.

tools & supplies
- Stitching Toolbox, p. 89
- Stringing Toolbox, p. 89
- split-ring pliers (optional)

techniques
- Russian spiral

DVD review ▶
Stitching Basics: Ending and Adding Thread

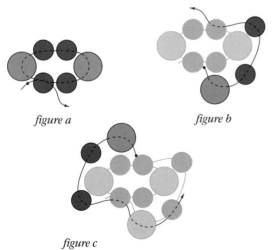

figure a

figure b

figure c

Design
option

Make it a multistrand. Make four or five 6-in. (15 cm) strands of Russian spiral using beads in a variety of complementary colors. String them on memory wire, separated by bead caps, for a fun bracelet.

Put it in reverse

Sheryl Yanagi transferred images to polymer clay, and then stitched bezels around the pieces to create a necklace that can be worn two ways. Simple neck strap strands won't compete with your fabulous centerpiece.

Polymer clay shapes

Condition each block of clay (Clays and Resin Basics p. 92), and wash your hands every time you switch clay colors.

1. Set the pasta machine to the thickest setting, and roll any color clay through it. Using shape cutters or the tissue blade, cut out a shape, such as a drop, circle, or leaf. Make as many shapes as desired.

2. Following the manufacturer's instructions, bake the shapes in the toaster oven. Allow the shapes to cool completely.

3. Using your finger, spread a thin, even layer of translucent liquid Sculpey polymer clay onto the sheet of glass or ceramic tile. Place your photocopy or laser-print image face down on the liquid Sculpey. Gently press the image into the liquid Sculpey, starting in the center and working out to remove any air pockets. Allow the image to rest for five minutes.

4. Following the manufacturer's instructions, bake the image on the sheet of glass or ceramic tile in the toaster oven. Remove the image from the oven while still hot, and slowly peel the paper away from the cured Sculpey. Gently peel the image transfer from the glass or ceramic tile, using a tissue blade if necessary, and lay it on a smooth surface to cool.

5. Trace each polymer clay shape onto the image transfer, or mark the image transfer by pressing the shape cutter into it. Cut out the shapes.

6. Using liquid Sculpey, glue each image transfer to each polymer clay shape **(photo 1)**, and bake in the toaster oven following the manufacturer's instructions. Remove the shapes, and let them cool completely.

Bezels

1. On 1 yd. (.9 m) of Fireline, pick up an even number of 11º cylinder beads to fit around a polymer clay shape, leaving a 12-in. (30 cm) tail. Tie the beads into a ring with a square knot (Stitching Basics, p. 89), and sew through the first few beads again.

2. Using cylinders, work in tubular peyote stitch (Stitching Basics) until you have a total of five rounds, and insert the polymer clay shape.

3. Adjusting your tension to snug the bezel around the polymer clay shape, work two rounds of tubular peyote with 15º seed beads. If desired, skip one or more stitches at the corner(s) to shape the bead-work: Sew through the next

bead in the previous round without adding a new bead; in the next round, pick up a bead over the skipped stitch. With the tail, repeat this step on the other side of the polymer clay shape. Tie a few half-hitch knots (Stitching Basics) to secure the working thread and tail, but do not trim.

4. Repeat steps 1–3 with the remaining polymer clay shapes. Repeat once more with a 10 mm fire-polished bead or round crystal (this will be the clasp bead), but cut 2 yd.

1

Image transfer tips

- Take great care during the image transfer process: Wipe away excess liquid Sculpey with a paper towel, and wash your hands. Alternatively, use a plastic knife or paintbrush to spread the liquid Sculpey onto the sheet of glass or ceramic tile. Use oven mitts to remove the glass or tile from the toaster oven, and allow the baked image to cool just enough to be able to touch it without burning your hands.
- Your image may stick to the paper instead of the cured Sculpey. Gently peel the paper off the Sculpey. Make extra copies of your image in case you need to redo the technique.
- A tissue blade helps to lift the transferred image from the sheet of glass or ceramic tile.

materials

necklace 16–24 in. (41–61 cm) with pendant 2¼ x 3 in. (5.7 x 7.6 cm)

- ¼–½ oz. polymer clay in each of **2**–**7** colors
- translucent liquid Sculpey polymer clay
- black-and-white photocopy or laser-print image (not ink-jet)
- 2–5 g 11º cylinder beads
- 4–7 g 15º seed beads
- **3** 10 mm fire-polished beads or round crystals
- **3** 8 mm fire-polished beads or round crystals
- Fireline 4 lb. test

tools & supplies

- Clays and Resin Toolbox, p. 92
- Stitching Toolbox, p. 89
- 3 x 5-in. (7.6 x 13 cm) sheet of glass or ceramic tile
- shape cutters (optional)

techniques

- polymer clay
- peyote stitch

DVD review ⏵

- Stitching: Square Knot, Half-Hitch Knot, Tubular Peyote Stitch
- Clays and Resin: Conditioning and Rolling Polymer Clay, Mixing Polymer Clay Colors

(1.8 m) of Fireline, and leave a 6-in. (15 cm) tail.

Pendant

1. Arrange your shapes as desired around an 8 mm fire-polished bead or round crystal.

2. To connect two shapes, sew through the beadwork to exit a cylinder in the center round of a bezel at the point where the two shapes touch. Sew through the corresponding cylinder in the center round of the other bezel and the cylinder your thread exited at the start of this step **(photo 2)**. Retrace the thread path a few times to secure the connection, and end the thread (Stitching Basics).

3. To connect shapes with an 8 mm, sew through the beadwork to exit a cylinder in the center round of a bezel. Pick up the 8 mm, sew through the corresponding cylinder(s) in the center round of the next bezel(s), and sew back through

the 8 mm and cylinder your thread exited at the start of this step **(photo 3)**. Retrace the thread path a few times, and end the thread.

Necklace

1. With the working thread of the 10 mm clasp bead, sew through the beadwork to exit a cylinder in the center round of the bezel. Pick up four 15ºs, an 8 mm, about 6–10 in. (15–25 cm) of 15ºs, and a 10 mm.

2. Sew through a cylinder in the center round of a clay shape bezel at the point where you want to attach your neck straps, and sew back through the 10 mm **(photo 4)**. Pick up

the same number of 15ºs as you picked up in step 1.

3. Sew through the 8 mm, four 15ºs, and the cylinder in the clasp bead bezel that your thread exited at the start of step 1. Sew back through the four 15ºs and 8 mm. Pick up the same number of 15ºs as in the first two strands **(photo 5)**. Sew through the 10 mm and the cylinder in the clay shape bezel. Retrace the thread path if desired, and end the thread.

4. On 1½–2 yd. (1.4–1.8 m) of Fireline, center enough 15ºs to make a loop for the clasp bead to fit through.

5. Over both threads, string an 8 mm. On each thread, pick up the same number of 15ºs as for the strands in step 1. Over both threads, string a 10 mm, and cross the threads through a cylinder in the center round of a clay shape bezel where you want the second neck strap to connect. Sew back through the 10 mm with both threads.

6. On one thread, pick up the same number of 15ºs as in the previous two strands, and sew through the 8 mm and loop of 15ºs from step 4. Retrace the thread path if desired, and end both threads.

Back

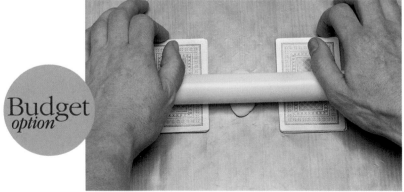

Pasta machine alternative. If you don't want to purchase a pasta machine or clay roller, simply roll out your polymer clay sheets with an acrylic roller. Make two stacks of five playing cards each, and tape each stack together. Place the playing card stacks on each side of your clay as guides for your roller.

Modern Art

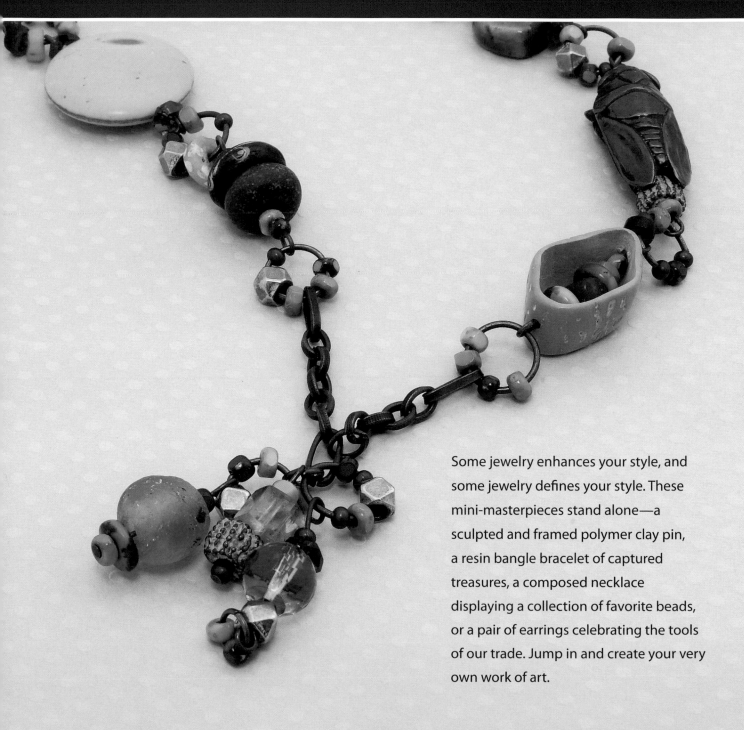

Some jewelry enhances your style, and some jewelry defines your style. These mini-masterpieces stand alone—a sculpted and framed polymer clay pin, a resin bangle bracelet of captured treasures, a composed necklace displaying a collection of favorite beads, or a pair of earrings celebrating the tools of our trade. Jump in and create your very own work of art.

Daring dangle

The small links in this silver-plated chain keep the embellishments of **Jane Konkel's** piece secure while the large links balance the design with an open, airy feel. You'll love the simplicity of making this bold architectural necklace almost as much as you'll love wearing it.

1. Cut a 16–18-in. (41–46 cm) piece of chain with a large link on each end. Cut a 4-in. (10 cm) piece of chain with a large link on one end and three small links on the other. Open the center large link of the long chain as you would a jump ring or loop (Stringing Basics, p. 89), and attach the three small links from the end of the short chain. Close the link. Remove a small link from each side of the center large link **(photo 1)**.

2. On a head pin, string a 10 mm glass pearl, and make a plain loop (Wirework Basics, p. 91). Make a total of two 10 mm units, two 8 mm units, and two 4 mm units, one each of colors A and B. Make four 6 mm units, two each of colors A and B.

3. Cut a 3-in. (7.6 cm) piece of 20-gauge wire. Make a plain loop on one end. String a color A 16 mm pearl, the top three small links of the short chain, and a color B 16 mm pearl. Make a plain loop. Open the loop of each 10 mm unit from step 2, and attach the plain loops made in this step, alternating pearl colors. Close the loops **(photo 2)**.

4. Using the 8–14 mm pearls and the bead units from step 2, repeat step 3 to make and attach pearls in descending sizes and alternating colors **(photo 3)**. You won't need as much wire as the pearls get smaller. Set aside one 8 mm and one 6 mm pearl for step 5.

5. On a head pin, string the remaining pearls, and make the first half of a wrapped loop (Wirework Basics). Attach one end of the long chain, and complete the wraps. On the other end, use a small link to attach a lobster claw clasp **(photo 4)**.

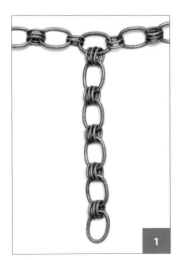

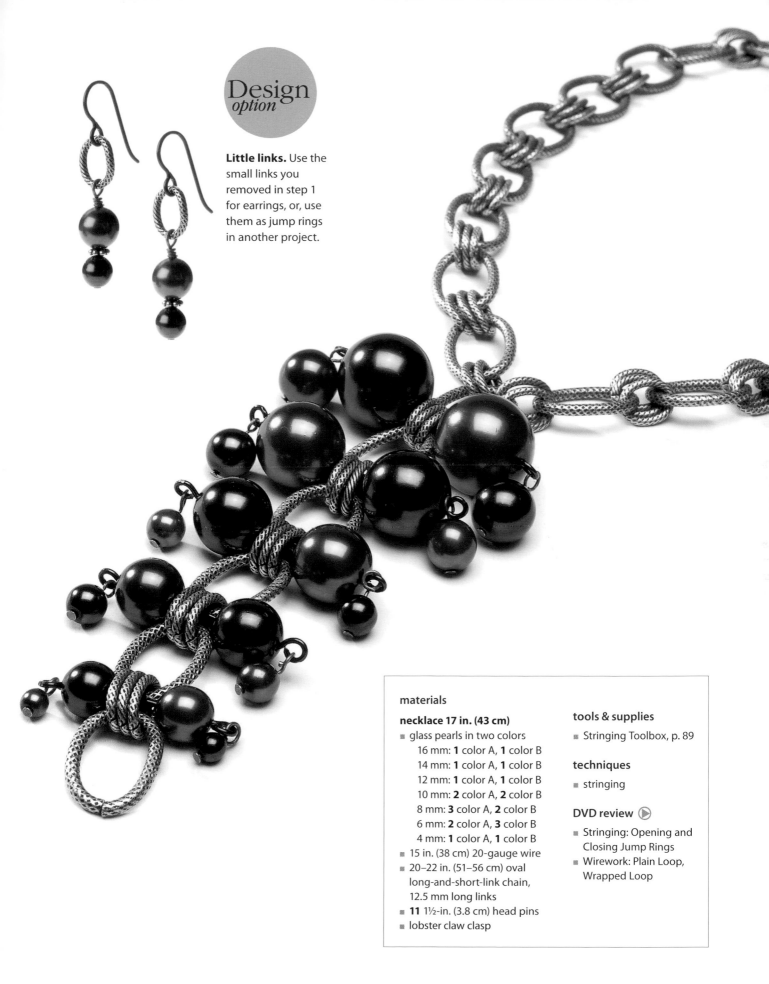

Design *option*

Little links. Use the small links you removed in step 1 for earrings, or, use them as jump rings in another project.

materials

necklace 17 in. (43 cm)

- glass pearls in two colors
    - 16 mm: **1** color A, **1** color B
    - 14 mm: **1** color A, **1** color B
    - 12 mm: **1** color A, **1** color B
    - 10 mm: **2** color A, **2** color B
    - 8 mm: **3** color A, **2** color B
    - 6 mm: **2** color A, **3** color B
    - 4 mm: **1** color A, **1** color B
- 15 in. (38 cm) 20-gauge wire
- 20–22 in. (51–56 cm) oval long-and-short-link chain, 12.5 mm long links
- **11** 1½-in. (3.8 cm) head pins
- lobster claw clasp

tools & supplies

- Stringing Toolbox, p. 89

techniques

- stringing

DVD review ▶

- Stringing: Opening and Closing Jump Rings
- Wirework: Plain Loop, Wrapped Loop

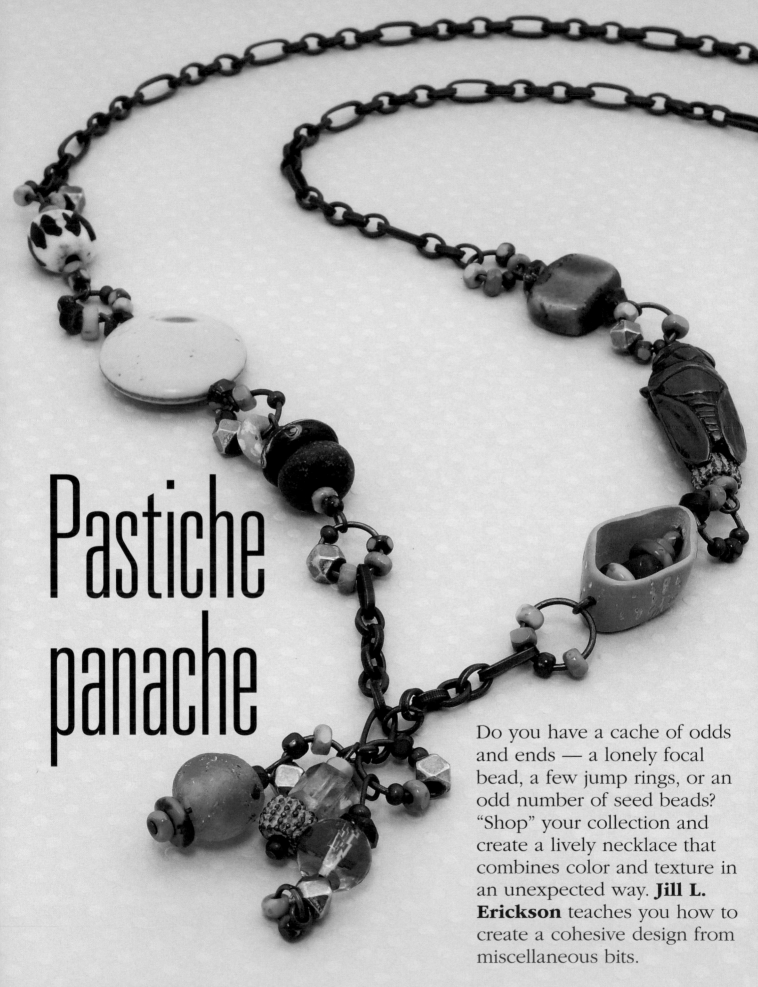

Pastiche panache

Do you have a cache of odds and ends — a lonely focal bead, a few jump rings, or an odd number of seed beads? "Shop" your collection and create a lively necklace that combines color and texture in an unexpected way. **Jill L. Erickson** teaches you how to create a cohesive design from miscellaneous bits.

Before you begin

Without a unifying element, eclectic and asymmetrical can turn into chaos. To keep your design cohesive, match the color and finish of your eye pins, head pins, jump rings, and clasp to your chain. That said, it's fine to use jump rings in various sizes because this adds just the right amount of unpredictability to your necklace.

Necklace

1. Make a bead unit: On an eye pin, string beads as desired, and make a plain loop (Wirework Basics, p. 91). Repeat to make a total of six bead units.

2. Open a large jump ring (Stringing Basics, p. 89), string two or three seed beads or other small beads, a loop of a bead unit, two or three seed beads, and a loop of another bead unit, and close the jump ring. Repeat to connect the six bead units with beaded jump rings to make two strands with three linked units each **(photo 1)**.

3. Cut 2 in. (5 cm) of chain. Open a large jump ring, embellish it as in step 2, and attach one end of the chain to one end of a three-unit strand. With another large jump ring, repeat to attach the other end of the chain to the other strand **(photo 2)**.

4. Make a head pin dangle: On a head pin, string beads as desired, and make a plain loop. Repeat to make a total of two head pin dangles.

5. Make an eye pin dangle: On an eye pin, string beads as desired, and make a plain loop. Open a small jump ring, string two or three seed beads and a loop of the eye pin, and close the jump ring.

6. Open a large jump ring, embellish it as in step 2, and attach a head pin dangle. Repeat with another large jump ring and the other head pin dangle. Find the center link of the 2-in. (5 cm) chain. Open a small jump ring, and attach one of the beaded jump ring components, the eye pin dangle, and the other beaded jump ring component **(photo 3)**.

7. Cut two 11-in. (28 cm) pieces of chain. Open a large jump ring, embellish it as in step 2, and attach the end unit of a three-unit strand and an end link of a chain **(photo 4)**. Repeat with the second piece of chain and the other strand.

8. Open a small jump ring. Attach a lobster claw clasp and the end link of a chain, and close the jump ring. Repeat on the other end, substituting a soldered jump ring for the clasp.

Earrings

For each earring: Open a large jump ring, and string a few seed beads or other small beads. Attach an earring finding, and close the jump ring.

Suit your style.
A complementary color palette unifies unique beads.

materials

necklace 25–30 in. (64–76 cm)
- 25–30 in. (64–76 cm) chain
- assorted beads, including at least **9** focals or accents (enough to make six bead units and three dangles)
- 50–75 6º three-cut seed beads or other small beads
- **7** 2-in. (5 cm) eye pins
- **2** 2-in. (5 cm) head pins
- **10** 8–12 mm (large) jump rings
- **4** 4–7 mm (small) jump rings
- lobster claw clasp and soldered jump ring

pair of earrings
- **2** 3–4 mm metal spacers
- **8** 6º three-cut seed beads or other small beads
- **2** 8–12 mm jump rings
- pair of earring findings

tools & supplies
- Wirework Toolbox, p. 91

techniques
- wirework

DVD review ▶
- Stringing: Opening and Closing Jump Rings
- Wirework: Plain Loop

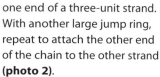

1

2

3

4

Step-by-step photos by Jill L. Erickson.

Check that the strands are about the same length. If needed, even things up by adding jump rings to the shorter strand. With an asymmetrical design, it's fine to mix things up a little.

Newfangled bangle

Fun and bright, these bracelets by **Sherri Haab** make great homes for your favorite beads and bits. Her first bangles were inspired by apple juice Bakelite bangles, which often include floral designs. Her collection of vintage plastic was well suited to fit nicely into a bangle mold. After you master the basic bangle, play with colorants to make striped layers.

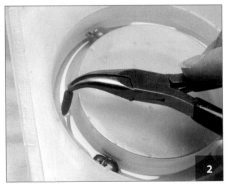

1. Following the manufacturer's directions, mix ½ ounce each of resin and hardener in a cup. Place the mold on a flat surface. Pour the resin into the bangle mold about half full **(photo 1)**. Briefly hold a heat gun over the resin to gently remove any bubbles. Use the heat gun again after a few minutes if any bubbles remain.

2. Wait until the resin thickens slightly, then place beads and found objects using pliers or tweezers **(photo 2)**. Allow to cure. You can speed the curing process by placing the mold near a 60- to 100-watt light bulb. Resin is fully cured when it is tack free and hard to the touch.

3. Mix ½ ounce each of resin and hardener in a cup and pour it into the mold. Add another layer of beads or found objects and allow to cure **(photo 3)**.

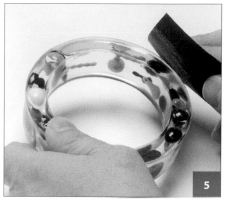

4. To remove the bangle, flex the mold and push on the back to gently loosen the bangle **(photo 4)**. Push the center of the mold inward (almost inside out) to free one of the edges.

5. To remove the rough edge at the top of the bangle, sand it with 200-grit sandpaper or an emery board **(photo 5)**.

6. Continue sanding the bangle in a bowl of water using wet/dry sandpapers. Sand the top and inside edges with 320-, 400-, 600-, 800-, 1000-, and 1200-grit papers, in that order **(photo 6)**. Use fresh water after each paper. Polish the bangle if desired (Polishing option, right).

materials

- **15–70** 4–20 mm beads or found objects
- EasyCast Clear Casting Epoxy
- bangle mold
- plastic gloves
- safety goggles
- chainnose or bentnose pliers or tweezers
- emery board, metal file, or 200-grit sandpaper
- heat gun
- wet/dry sandpapers in 320-, 400-, 600-, 800-, 1000-, and 1200-grits
- buffing compounds (optional)
- lathe and muslin buffing wheels (optional)

Bangle mold, buffing compounds, lathe, and muslin buffing wheels from sherrihaab.com.

tools & supplies

- Clays and Resin Toolbox, p. 92

techniques

- resin

DVD review ▶

- Clays and Resin: Using Resin

• *To avoid bubbles, warm the resin and hardener before working. Set the bottles under a light bulb or in a warm place.*

• *If you use large (20 mm) beads, make sure they're flat; otherwise they won't fit in the bangle.*

• *In step 2, make sure to wait until the resin has thickened before you add beads or objects. If you add them too soon, they'll sink to the bottom.*

• *The mold is reusable, so flex it back into shape after removing the bracelet.*

Polishing option

For a crystal clear finish, use buffing compounds on a muslin wheel. Start with a cutting compound and a stitched wheel at a low speed (1000–1500 rpm). Use an unstitched wheel with a polishing compound for a final buff. For more information, visit foredom.net.

Turn cartwheels for pinwheels

Bristle disks hold a strange fascination for **Hazel L. Wheaton** and she was inspired to use them as jewelry-making ingredients. Designed to be used in a flex shaft for polishing metal, the pinwheel-shaped disks are sold in sets of six different grits. Each grit has its own distinct, bright color. Back these bristles with a metal disk and add a simple spiral earring finding, and you'll have a pair of earrings in record time!

1. Choose your metal disk size; my bristle disks are ¾ in. (1.9 cm), so I used metal disks in the same size. You can buy pre-cut disks, but it's easy to cut your own: Slide 20-gauge (0.81 mm) copper sheet into a disk cutter. Use a brass mallet to strike the appropriate-size punch to cut out the disk (**photo 1**). Strike as few times as needed — it'll make a cleaner cut. Repeat to cut out a second disk.

2. Place coarse-grit sandpaper on your work surface, and use your fingers to move each disk over the sandpaper in a figure-8 pattern to smooth the disks' edges (**photo 2**).

3. Set a bristle disk on a copper disk, and mark the placement of the bristle disk's hole. Use heavy-duty hole-punching pliers to make a hole in the disk **(photo 3)**. Repeat to make a hole in the second disk.

4. Cut a 6-in. (15 cm) piece of 20-gauge copper wire. Using flatnose pliers, make a 90-degree bend 2 in. (5 cm) from one end of the wire **(photo 4)**. Using roundnose pliers, make a loop in the short end of the wire above the bend **(photo 5)**. Make a spiral around the loop **(photo 6)** with two full rotations. Trim the end of

the wire **(photo 7)**. Repeat this step to make a second spiral.

5. String two bristle disks and a copper disk onto the tail of one spiral. (Make sure the bristles of the bristle disks point in opposing directions.) Hold the disks tight together, then pull the wire tail up flat against the back of the copper disk **(photo 8)**.

6. Using forming pliers, grip the wire tail above the rim of the disks, and bend it slightly

forward **(photo 9)**. Reposition the forming pliers, and wrap the tail backward over the largest jaw of the pliers **(photo 10)**. With your fingers, bend the end of the tail outward slightly, then use sandpaper to smooth the end of the wire. Repeat steps 5 and 6 for the second spiral.

7. Place each ear wire flat on a bench block or anvil. Use a chasing hammer to flatten the curve slightly and work-harden the wire.

Bristle disks wear down and get dirty with use. To clean them, just soak them in a solution of dish soap and water for 10–15 minutes, then rinse them well, and let them dry. Repeat if necessary.

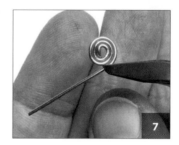

Design *option*

Mod metal. Cut metal disks that are larger than the bristle disks to create a border around the pinwheels. Or, try using silver instead of copper, or use a different shape — many suppliers sell pre-cut metal shapes, often called "stamping disks." Lillypilly Designs (lillypillydesigns.com) even sells them in cool shades and patterns in anodized aluminum.

Rolling tide

Picture a microscopic beach with sea foam bubbles, lapping waves, and the midday sun reflecting off the water. **Lori Wilkes** transforms this image into a stunning polymer clay brooch.

materials

pin

- 4–6 mm freshwater pearl (preferably flat on one side)
- 1 oz. polymer clay in each of 2 colors: white and rhino gray (Premo)
- liquid polymer clay
- pin-back finding

tools & supplies

- Clays and Resin Toolbox, p. 92
- mesh texture sheet or bag
- clay ball tool
- clay extruder with template disks (Makins)
- colored chalks (EKSuccess)
- glue (Crafter's Pick: The Ultimate!)
- watercolor paints (multiple colors)
- sponge sanding block, fine

technique

- polymer clay

DVD review

- Clays and Resin: Conditioning and Rolling Polymer Clay, Mixing Polymer Clay Colors

---

- *If you don't have a pasta machine, use the acrylic roller or brayer to roll a sheet of clay about ¹/₁₆ in. (2 mm) thick in step 1.*
- *You may need to use a needle tool to place the strands onto the clay in step 5.*
- *I used scrapbooking chalks in pastel colors in step 9.*
- *If your pin-back finding has prongs, set them before curing the clay.*
- *I used a mesh vegetable bag for my mesh texture.*

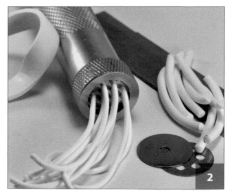

1. Condition the white and gray clays (Clays and Resin Basics, p. 92). Set the pasta machine to the thickest setting and roll a sheet of gray clay about 2½ x 2½ in. (6.4 x 6.4 cm). Using the tissue blade, cut the clay to roughly the desired size and shape brooch. Place the clay on top of the mesh, and use the acrylic roller or brayer to gently impress the texture into the back surface **(photo 1)**.

2. Fill the extruder with the remaining gray clay. Fit the extruder with the small rectangle disk, and extrude a 7-in. (18 cm) strip of gray clay. Set it aside for step 10. Empty the extruder, load it with white clay, and fit the extruder with the wide

rectangle disk. Extrude an 8-in. (20 cm) strip of clay. Replace the disk with the seven-circle disk, and extrude 3 in. (7.6 cm) of clay. Replace the disk with the four-circle disk, and extrude 3 in. (7.6 cm) of clay **(photo 2)**.

3. Using the acrylic roller or brayer, roll along the 8- in. (20 cm) strip of white clay **(photo 3)**.

4. Cut the white strip into four 2- in. (5 cm) sections. Cut the round strands into varying lengths between ¹/₁₆ and ³/₁₆ in. (2–5 mm). Using a paintbrush, apply liquid polymer clay to the untextured side of the gray clay sheet made in step 1 **(photo 4)**.

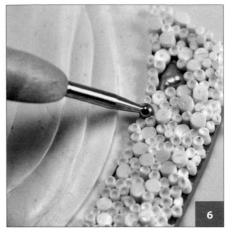

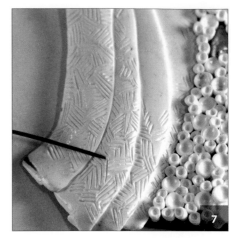

6. Using a clay ball tool, gently make depressions on the top of each strand **(photo 6)**.

7. Using a needle tool, gently scratch the layered strips with crosshatch marks **(photo 7)**.

8. Trim the excess clay from the edges with the tissue blade **(photo 8)**.

9. Using a dry paintbrush, apply colored chalks to the clay as desired **(photo 9)**.

10. Apply a thin coat of liquid polymer clay around the edges of the brooch. Starting on the bottom edge, carefully wrap the gray strip from step 2 around the brooch **(photo 10)**. Trim the strip ends flush, and gently press the seam to blend.

11. Mix blue and gray watercolors, and apply a watercolor wash over the cross-hatch marks and strands **(photo 11)**. Let the watercolor dry completely.

12. Bake the clay following the manufacturer's instructions, and let it cool completely. Using a fine sanding block, sand the edges of the clay. Glue the pin-back finding to the back of the clay, and let it dry completely.

5. Overlap the flattened white strips in a staggered pattern along one edge of the gray clay **(photo 5)**. Place the pearl on the gray clay in an offset position, and gently press it into the clay. Add the cut round strands around it. The strands will act as prongs, so position them close enough to hold the pearl in place. Randomly place the wider strands on the remaining surface, and fill between them with the narrower strands.

Basics

Go to the *Stylish Jewelry* DVD to watch videos of the techniques that have this symbol ▶ next to them.

Stringing In stringing, there are only a few basics to master and a few tools to use.

Stringing Toolbox:

Tape measure; padded work surface or bead design board; wire cutters; crimping pliers; roundnose pliers; at least two pairs of chainnose, flatnose, and/or bentnose pliers

Stringing Basics:

Cutting flexible beading wire

Decide the length of your necklace or bracelet. Add 6 in. (15 cm) for a necklace or 5 in. (13 cm) for a bracelet, and cut a piece of beading wire to that length. The additional length allows room for finishing.

▶ Crimping

Use crimp beads to finish the ends of flexible beading wire with either a flattened or a folded crimp. To make a flattened crimp, slide the crimp bead into place, and squeeze it firmly with chainnose

pliers. For a more finished look, make a folded crimp:

1. Position the crimp bead in the hole that is closest to the handle of the crimping pliers.
2. Holding the wires apart, squeeze the pliers to compress the crimp bead, making sure one wire is on each side of the dent.
3. Place the crimp bead in the front hole of the pliers, and position it so the dent is facing the tips of the pliers. Squeeze the pliers to fold the crimp in half.
4. Tug on the wires to ensure that the crimp is secure.

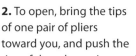

Opening and closing loops or jump rings

1. Hold each side of a loop or a jump ring with a pair of pliers, such as chainnose, flatnose, or bentnose.
2. To open, bring the tips of one pair of pliers toward you, and push the tips of the other pair away from you. Reverse the steps to close the open loop or jump ring.

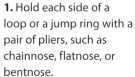

▶ BONUS! COVER YOUR CRIMPS

For polished finishing, watch a demonstration of using crimp covers on the DVD.

Stitching Sew with a needle and thread through seed beads, crystals, and other beads in regular stitch patterns.

Stitching Toolbox:

Tape measure; padded work surface; scissors; #10 and #12 beading needles; thread conditioner, such as Thread Heaven or microcrystalline wax

Stitching Basics:

Threading a needle

Cut the length of thread indicated. Hold one end of the thread with your non-dominant hand. With your dominant hand, slide the eye of the needle over the end of the thread.

Conditioning thread

Use beeswax or microcrystalline wax (not candle wax or paraffin) or Thread Heaven to condition nylon beading thread and Fireline. Wax smooths nylon fibers and

adds tackiness that will stiffen the beadwork slightly. Thread Heaven adds a static charge that causes the thread to repel itself, so don't use it with doubled thread. Both conditioners help nylon thread and Fireline resist wear.

To condition, stretch nylon thread to remove the curl (you don't need to stretch Fireline). Lay the thread or Fireline on top of the conditioner, hold it in place with your thumb or finger, and pull the thread through the conditioner.

▶ Ending and adding thread

To end a thread, sew back through the last few rows or rounds of beadwork, following the existing thread path and tying a few half-hitch knots (see "Half-hitch knot") between beads as you go. Sew through

a few beads after the last knot, and trim the thread.

To add a new thread, sew into the beadwork several rows or rounds prior to where the last stitch ended, leaving a short tail. Follow the existing thread path, tying a few half-hitch knots (see "Half-hitch knot") between beads, and exit where the last stitch ended. Trim the short tail.

Half-hitch knot

Pass the needle under the thread bridge between two beads, and pull gently until a loop forms. Cross back over the thread between the beads, sew through the loop, and pull gently to draw the knot into the beadwork.

Overhand knot

Make a loop with the thread. Pull the tail through the loop, and tighten.

Square knot

1. Cross one end of the thread over and under the other end. Pull both ends to tighten the first half of the knot.
2. Cross the first end of the thread over and under the other end. Pull both ends to tighten the knot.

Surgeon's knot

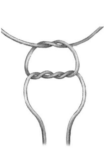

1. Cross one end of the thread over and under the other twice. Pull both ends to tighten the first half of the knot.
2. Cross the first end of the thread over and under the other end. Pull both ends to tighten the knot.

Attaching a stop bead

Use a stop bead to secure beads temporarily when you begin stitching. Choose a bead that is different from the beads in your project. Pick up the stop bead, leaving the desired length tail. Sew through the stop bead again in the same direction, making sure you don't split the thread. If desired, sew through it one more time for added security.

Ladder stitch

1. Pick up two beads, and sew through them both again, positioning the beads side by side so that their holes are parallel **(a–b)**.

2. Add subsequent beads by picking up one bead, sewing through the previous bead, then sewing through the new bead **(b–c)**. Continue for the desired length ladder.

This technique produces uneven tension, which you can correct by zigzagging back through the beads in the opposite direction.

Herringbone stitch

1. Work the first row in ladder stitch (see "Ladder stitch") to the desired length, exiting the top of the last bead added.
2. Pick up two beads, and sew down through the next bead in the previous row **(a–b)**. Sew up through the following bead in the previous row, pick up two beads, and sew down through the next bead **(b–c)**. Repeat across the first row.

3. To turn to start the next row, sew down through the end bead in the previous row and back through the last bead of the pair just added **(a–b)**. Pick up two beads, sew down through the next bead in the previous row, and sew up through the following bead **(b–c)**. Continue adding pairs of beads across the row.

To turn without having thread show on the edge, pick up an accent or smaller bead before you sew back through the last bead of the pair you just added, or work a concealed turn: Sew up through the second-to-last bead in the previous row, and continue through the last bead added **(a–b)**. Pick up two beads, sew down through the next bead in the previous row, and sew up through the following bead **(b–c)**. Continue adding pairs of beads across the row. Using this turn will straighten out the angle of the edge beads, making the edge stacks look a little different than the others.

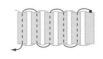

Flat even-count peyote stitch

1. Pick up an even number of beads, leaving the desired length tail **(a–b)**. These beads will shift to form the first two rows as the third row is added.

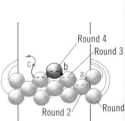

2. To begin row 3, pick up a bead, skip the last bead added in the previous step, and sew back through the next bead, working toward the tail **(b–c)**. For each stitch, pick up a bead, skip a bead in the previous row, and sew through the next bead until you reach the first bead picked up in step 1 **(c–d)**. The beads added in this row are higher than the previous rows and are referred to as "up-beads."
3. For each stitch in subsequent rows, pick up a bead, and sew through the next up-bead in the previous row **(d–e)**. To count peyote stitch rows, count the total number of beads along both straight edges.

Tubular peyote stitch

Tubular peyote stitch follows the same stitching pattern as flat even-count peyote stitch, but instead of sewing back and forth, you work in rounds.
1. Start with an even number of beads tied into a ring (see "Square knot" or "Surgeon's knot").
2. Sew through the first bead in the ring. Pick up a bead, skip a bead in the ring, and sew through the next bead. Repeat to complete the round.
3. To step up to start the next round, sew through the first bead added in round 3 **(a–b)**. Pick up a bead, and sew through the next bead in round 3 **(b–c)**. Repeat to achieve the desired length, stepping up after each round.

Zipping up peyote stitch

To join two sections of a flat peyote piece invisibly, match up the two pieces so the end rows fit together.

"Zip up" the pieces by zigzagging through the up-beads on both ends.

▶ Right-angle weave

1. To start the first row of right-angle weave, pick up four beads, and tie them into a ring (see "Square knot" or "Surgeon's knot"). Sew through the first three beads again.

2. Pick up three beads. Sew through the last bead in the previous stitch (**a–b**), and continue through the first two beads picked up in this stitch (**b–c**).

3. Continue adding three beads per stitch until the first row is the desired length. You are stitching in a figure-8 pattern, alternating the direction of the thread path for each stitch.

4. To begin the next row, sew through the last stitch of row 1, exiting an edge bead along one side.

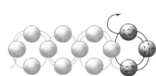

5. Pick up three beads, and sew through the edge bead your thread exited in the previous step (**a–b**). Continue through the first new bead (**b–c**).

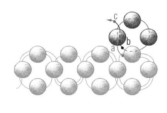

6. Pick up two beads, and sew back through the next edge bead in the previous row and the bead your thread exited at the start of this step (**a–b**). Continue through the two new beads and the following edge bead in the previous row (**b–c**).

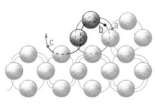

7. Pick up two beads, and sew through the last two beads your thread exited in the previous stitch and the first new bead. Continue working a figure-8 thread path, picking up two beads per stitch for the rest of the row.

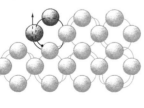

Wirework Bend, wrap, spiral, texture, hammer, or otherwise form wire with your hands or pliers to make jewelry.

Wirework Toolbox:

Tape measure; wire cutters; roundnose pliers; nylon-jaw pliers; at least two pairs of chainnose, flatnose, and/or bentnose pliers; chasing hammer; ball-peen hammer; steel bench block or anvil; cup bur or wire rounder; polishing cloth; liver of sulfur (optional)

Wirework Basics:

▶ Plain loop

1. Using chainnose or flatnose pliers, make a right-angle bend in the wire directly above a bead or other component or at least ¼ in. (6 mm) from the end of a naked piece of wire. For a larger loop, bend the wire farther in.

2. Grip the end of the wire with roundnose pliers so that the wire is flush with the jaws of the pliers where they meet. The closer to the tip of the pliers that you work, the smaller the loop will be. Press downward slightly, and rotate the wire toward the bend made in step 1.

3. Reposition the pliers in the loop to continue rotating the wire until the end of the wire touches the bend.

▶ Wrapped loop

1. Using chainnose or flatnose pliers, make a right-angle bend in the wire about 2 mm above a bead or other component or at least 1¼ in. (3.2 cm) from the end of a naked piece of wire.

2. Position the jaws of the roundnose pliers in the bend. The closer to the tip of the pliers that you work, the smaller the loop will be.

3. Curve the short end of the wire over the top jaw of the roundnose pliers.

4. Reposition the pliers so the lower jaw fits snugly in the loop. Curve the wire downward around the bottom jaw of the pliers. This is the first half of a wrapped loop.

5. To complete the wraps, grasp the top of the loop with chainnose or flatnose pliers.

6. With another pair of chainnose or flatnose pliers, wrap the wire around the stem two or three times. Trim the excess wire, and gently press the cut end close to the wraps with chainnose pliers.

Coiling wire

Wire can be wrapped around a mandrel or other core to make a coil, which may be decorative, functional, or both. Wire-coiling tools like the Coiling Gizmo make this fast and easy, but for small jobs or when you're coiling directly onto a wire that you'll use in your project, you can do it by hand: Hold the coiling wire perpendicular to the core or mandrel. Wrap the wire around the core until the coil is the desired length. Keep the wraps close to each other to prevent gaps in the coil.

▶ BONUS! MAKE YOUR OWN FINDINGS
Learn how to make wirework earring findings and S-hook clasps on the DVD.

Metalwork

Cut shapes, rivet metal together, add texture, or apply a surface patina—the options in metalworking are wide and varied.

Metalwork Toolbox:

Tape measure; metal shears; chasing hammer; ball-peen hammer; rawhide mallet; steel bench block or anvil; hand files; needle files; sandpaper or sanding pads, various grits; brass brush; 0000 steel wool; polishing papers; polishing cloth; liver of sulfur (optional); cross-locking tweezers (optional); tumbler with steel shot, burnishing compound, and sieve (optional); butane torch (optional)

Metalwork Basics:

Cutting metal with shears

Shears can take several forms. A bench shear is a single-bladed tool; it looks like a heavy-duty paper cutter and works the same way. The bench shear is mounted on a sturdy, stable surface and works best for cutting straight edges through sheet metal. For smaller jobs, handheld shears work well; most craft supply stores and hardware stores sell these. Be sure to check the maximum gauge that a pair of shears can handle. Most handheld shears can cut through metal up to 22-gauge, and some manufacturers make spring-loaded shears for heavier gauges.

As you cut, the metal will bend slightly away from the shears; the thicker the metal, the more it will bend. Place your cut-out piece on a steel bench block, and hammer it lightly with a rawhide mallet to flatten it. Also, run your finger lightly along the cut edge to detect any burrs or uneven spots. If necessary, use a file or coarse-grit sandpaper to smooth the edge.

▶ Adding a patina with liver of sulfur

Polish your piece before patinating. (If you tumble-polish your piece after patinating, reserve the used shot for future patinated pieces; the liver of sulfur residue will contaminate non-patinated pieces.) Oil and dirt on the piece can affect the patina, so clean the metal with degreasing soap before patinating.

Prepare a liver of sulfur solution according to the manufacturer's instructions. Dip the metal in the solution for a few seconds, then rinse in cool water to stop the chemical reaction. For a darker patina, continue to dip and rinse the metal. Use a brass brush with soapy water to remove or modify the patina. By varying the temperature and amount of water you use to make the solution, you can achieve different colors of patina; experiment to find the result you prefer.

▶ Balling up the end of a wire

Using cross-locking tweezers or pliers, grasp a piece of wire at its midpoint, and dip the wire in flux. Hold the wire vertically, and lower one end of the wire into the tip of the inner blue cone of your butane torch's flame. After a ball forms at the end of the wire, remove the flame, then quench, rinse, and dry the wire.

Tumble polishing

Place steel shot into the tumbler's barrel. You can use any shape of steel shot, but a combination of shapes works best. The various shapes polish crevices and contours differently, for an even polish.

Pour in enough water to cover the shot, then add a pinch of burnishing compound. Place your jewelry in the tumbler, and seal the barrel. Turn on the tumbler, and let it run for two to three hours or more. Pour the contents of the tumbler into a sieve over a sink, and rinse. Remove your jewelry, and dry it. Dry the shot before storing it.

▶ BONUS! USING A DISK CUTTER

Learn how to cut perfect metal circles using a disk cutter on the DVD.

Clays and Resin

Roll, stamp, shape, and sculpt **metal clay** in ways not possible with standard sheet metal. With **polymer clay**, blend colors, shape and form, add inlays, apply image transfers and more. **Resin**, a two-part epoxy, can be layered, poured into a mold, used as a coating, or colored.

Clays and Resin Toolbox:

Tape measure; nonstick work surface; latex/nitrile gloves; airtight storage containers; distilled water; spray bottle; plastic wrap; sponges or paper towels; playing cards or clay thickness guides; acrylic roller or PVC pipe; craft knife, scalpel, and/or tissue blade; texture sheets; sponge applicators and/or fine-tip paintbrushes; needle tool; smoothing tool; needle files; wet/dry sandpaper, various grits; nail buff or emery board; brass brush; burnisher; tweezers

Tools specific to metal clay: olive oil or natural hand balm; handheld butane torch with firing brick or kiln with kiln shelf

Tools specific to polymer clay: clay-dedicated pasta machine; clay-dedicated toaster oven; oven thermometer; smooth ceramic baking surface

Tools specific to resin: clear plastic medicine cups for measuring and mixing resin; wooden craft sticks; plastic garbage bags

Clays and Resin Basics:

▶ Conditioning polymer clay

All polymer clay must be conditioned before you work with it. To prepare stiffer clays for conditioning, warm them by placing the unopened package on a heating pad set to low, or seal the package in a plastic bag and set it in a bowl of warm water.

To condition clay by hand, roll the clay into a ball, flatten it, and roll it into a snake. Fold the snake in half, twist it, and roll it into a ball again. Repeat until the clay is soft and pliable.

Polymer clay can also be conditioned with a pasta machine. Adjust the machine

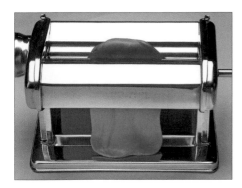

to its thickest setting, flatten one end of the clay with your hand, and run it through the machine. Fold the sheet of clay in half, and run the clay through the machine again, folded side first. Use a needle tool to puncture any air pockets that form. Continue to fold the clay (in the same direction each time), and run it through the machine until it's soft and pliable.

▶ BONUS! MIXING MULTIPLE POLYMER CLAY COLORS
Discover how to customize your clay colors on the DVD.

▶ Rolling metal clay
Metal clay dries rapidly, so remove from the package only the amount you will use during a given work session. Store unused clay in an airtight container with a small piece of moist sponge or paper towel. Cover clay with plastic wrap while you are not working with it. Use a spray bottle to remoisten the clay if it begins to dry out.

Apply olive oil or natural hand balm to your hands, tools, and work surface to prevent the clay from sticking. Decide how

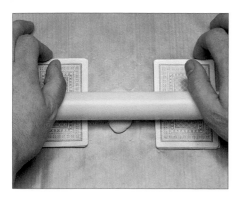

thick you want your metal clay sheet to be. Make two stacks of playing cards or thickness guides that equal that thickness. Place your lump of clay on your work surface between the two even stacks. Using an acrylic roller or PVC pipe, roll the clay to a uniform thickness. Rotate the clay 90 degrees, and roll it again.

▶ Cutting metal clay
Metal clay can be cut with a tissue blade, scalpel, or craft knife (such as an X-acto knife). To create a uniformly curved edge, bend a tissue blade into the desired curve, and press it down into the clay.

▶ Texturing metal clay
Apply a light coat of olive oil or natural hand balm to the surface of a texture sheet and to an acrylic roller or PVC pipe. Follow

the instructions for "Rolling metal clay" to make a sheet of clay. Place the texture sheet texture side up between two even stacks of cards or thickness guides. Lay the sheet of clay on the texture sheet. Using the roller, roll over the clay sheet. Carefully peel the clay from the texture sheet.

▶ Torch-firing metal clay with a butane torch
Metal clay pieces must be under 25 g in weight and the size of a United States silver dollar or smaller in order to be torch-fired. Firing time ranges from one to five minutes, depending on the weight of the piece (see the Torch-Firing Times chart, above).
1. Place the unfired metal clay in the middle of a firing brick.
2. Hold the torch at a 45-degree angle about 2 in. (5 cm) from the piece, and ignite the torch.
3. You will see a small amount of smoke and flame, and the piece will turn white. Keep the torch moving over the piece until

TORCH-FIRING TIMES

Weight (grams)	Time (minutes)
1–5	1
6–10	1½
11–15	2
16–20	2½–3
21–25	3½–5

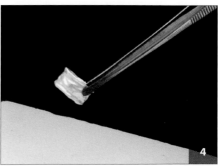

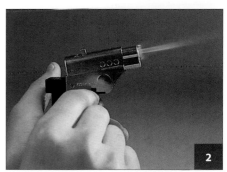

it glows. When the piece turns a peach color, begin timing. Increase or decrease the torch distance from the metal clay depending on whether the color intensifies or fades. If the piece begins to look shiny or if you see sparks, the piece is near the melting point; pull the torch farther away. **4.** After firing, use tweezers to move your piece to the cooler edge of the firing brick, and allow it to cool completely.

▶ **BONUS!**
FILLING A
BUTANE TORCH
See how to fill a butane torch on the DVD.

▶ **Using resin**
Cover your work surface with plastic bags or waxed paper to make spills easy to clean up. Baby wipes or a paper towel with rubbing alcohol will remove resin from unprotected work surfaces, but check the manufacturer's instructions for recommended clean-up solvents.

Remove any watches, rings, or other jewelry that could come in contact with wet resin. Keep your hands clean as you work to avoid leaving fingerprints.

Mix resin in clear plastic medicine cups. Different brands require different mixing ratios; read the manufacturer's instructions carefully. To make the liquid volume measurements indicated on the cup more visible, mark the desired measurement on the cup with a permanent marker first. And remember: Once the two parts of the resin are combined, the clock starts ticking.

Until fully cured, resin can pick up dust, pet hair, and small objects. Place a clean box, bowl, or plasticware container over your pieces while they cure.

Notice some imperfections? Most resin scratches and scrapes can be fixed by applying a fresh topcoat.

Use many techniques to turn your piece into jewelry, but play it safe: Even if a resin is labeled nontoxic, that may only refer to the wet and/or cured stages. Check manufacturer recommendations before sanding, sawing, or drilling any cured resin pieces.

Stylish Jewelry
Your Way

DVD
INDEX

RUN TIME 77 min.

Brush up on
28 **essential techniques:**

Stringing

Crimping

Using Crimp Covers

Opening and Closing Jump Rings

Wirework

Plain Loop

Wrapped Loop

Making Your Own Earring Wires

Making Your Own S-Hook Clasp

Stitching

Ending and Adding Thread and
   Making a Half-hitch Knot

Overhand Knot

Square Knot

Surgeon's Knot

Ladder Stitch

Flat Herringbone Stitch

Flat Peyote Stitch

Peyote Stitch, Joining Ends

Tubular Peyote Stitch

Flat Right Angle Weave

Metalwork

Adding Patina with Liver of Sulfur

Balling the End of a Wire

Using a Disk Cutter

Clays and Resin

Conditioning and Rolling
   Polymer Clay

Mixing Polymer Clay Colors

Rolling and Cutting Metal Clay

Texturing Metal Clay

Torch-Firing Metal Clay

Filling a Butane Torch

Using Resin

Contributors

Theresa D. Abelew lives in Milwaukee with her husband, daughter, and their rescued pets. When she is not working on a variety of projects in her studio, she can be found performing with one of her fire dance troupes. Theresa is editorial associate for *Art Jewelry*. Reach her in care of the magazine.

Linda Augsburg is a freelance editor and quilt designer. She runs Farmandcitystampin.com from the farmhouse where she was raised. She makes time to create jewelry for herself, family, and friends. Reach her at farmandcitystampin@gmail.com.

Lisa Barth has been a creative person all her life. A certified metal clay instructor and wire jewelry artist in Atlanta, Ga., she began designing wire jewelry in 2003. Contact Lisa at ibelisab@yahoo.com, or visit her website, lbjewelrydesigns.com.

Tea Benduhn is a former associate editor for *Bead&Button*. Contact her in care of Kalmbach Books.

Jane Danley Cruz has been beading for more than 20 years. She is an associate editor for *Bead&Button*. Contact her at jcruz@beadandbutton.com.

Anna Elizabeth Draeger is a well-known jewelry designer, former associate editor for *Bead&Button*, and the author of *Crystal Brilliance, Great Designs for Shaped Beads*, and *Crystal Play*. Since 2009, Anna has been an ambassador for Create Your Style with Swarovski Elements, a handpicked worldwide network of artists known for their design expertise and passion for teaching. Her website is originaldesignsbyanna.squarespace.com

Jill L. Erickson is a former associate editor for Art Jewelry magazine and now a full-time maker and teacher. She leads a popular class in the fundamentals of polymer at the annual Bead&Button Show.

Diane Fitzgerald is an internationally recognized teacher, designer, and author. Among her numerous awards, she received the Spun Gold Award from the Textile Center of Minnesota for her lifetime commitment to fiber art. Diane has written 12 beading books including her most recent, *Shaped Beadwork and Beyond*. Diane teaches classes at many locations, listed on her website at dianefitzgerald.com.

Naomi Fujimoto is editor of *Bead Style* magazine and author of *Cool Jewels: Beading Projects for Teens*. Visit her at cooljewelsbynaomi@etsy.com. Reach her in care of *Bead Style*.

Julia Gerlach is the editor of *Bead&Button* magazine. Contact her at jgerlach@kalmbach.com.

Sherri Haab is a best-selling craft author with over 23 published books to her credit, with several selling over a million copies each. Visit her website, sherrihaab.com.

Melanie Hazen is a part-time jewelry and glass artist working in Cumberland City, Tenn. Contact her via email at melaniehazen@mac.com, or visit melaniehazen.etsy.com.

Cathy Jakicic is the author of the books *Jewelry Projects from a Beading Insider* and *Hip Handmade Memory Jewelry*. She is the former editor of *Bead Style*, and has been creating jewelry for more than 15 years. Contact her at cathyjakicic@att.net.

Jane Konkel is a former associate editor of *Bead Style*. Contact her in care of Kalmbach Books.

Kelsey Lawler is assistant editor of *Bead Style*. Contact her at klawler@beadstylemag.com

Susan Lenart Kazmer is an internationally acclaimed mixed-media artist and silversmith of 25 years and has exhibited work in the Smithsonian, Art Institute of New York, and other venues. Susan was an originating founder of the Greater Chicago Bead Society. She is the originator of a successful commercial craft line of jewelry called Industrial Chic, and her second book is *Resin Alchemy*. Susan is the president and creative director of ICE Resin/SLK LLC, an artist-based manufacturing company for jewelry and mixed media.

Irina Miech is an artist, teacher, and the author of nine books on jewelry making. She also oversees her retail bead supply business and classroom studio, Eclectica and The Bead Studio in Brookfield, Wis., where she teaches classes in beading, wirework, and metal clay. Contact Irina at Eclectica, 262-641-0910, or via email at eclecticainfo@sbcglobal.net.

Cynthia Murray comments on her jewelry-making journey at cynthiamurraydesign.blogspot.com.

Kim Otterbein has been surrounded by beads her entire life. Living above a bead store gives her lots of gemstones, pearls, crystals, and glass to choose from, but as she puts it,"You can be just as creative using your stash of leftover beads." Contact Kim at The Bead House, 401-253-1188, or at info@thebeadhouse.com.

Contact **Kriss Silva** in care of Kalmbach Books.

Contact **Leanne Elliott Soden** at leannesoden@comcast.net.

Kim St. Jean combines her love of teaching with her creative talent as a jewelry maker. She teaches metalworking and other jewelry-making techniques at an array of venues across the U.S. and, when she's not traveling, at her studio in Myrtle Beach, S.C. Kim is the author of *Mixed Metal Mania* and *Metal Magic*. Contact her via email at kim@kimstjean.com, or through her website, kimstjean.com.

Contact **Toni Taylor** via email at toni269@gmail.com, or visit her website, tonitaylor.com.

Stacy Werkheiser is an associate editor at *Bead&Button* magazine and a recent issue editor of *Wirework* magazine. Contact her at swerkheiser@kalmbach.com.

Hazel L. Wheaton, editor of *Art Jewelry* magazine, can be reached at hwheaton@kalmbach.com.

Lori Wilkes is an artist, author, and instructor living in the midwest. She's originally from New England, and many of her designs are inspired by her coastal childhood. Lori is the author of *The Absolute Beginners Guide: Working with Polymer Clay*. Her jewelry designs have been featured in many books and magazines. Visit her website at millori.com.

Sheryl Yanagi channels her detail-oriented skills as a computer programmer into the detailed beadwork she designs. Her beads of choice are 15° seed beads, though she admits to being obsessively attracted to all things bright and shiny. Contact Sheryl at syanagi@comcast.net.

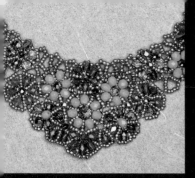